Riding off the Edge of the Map

Riding off the Edge of the Map

David Bryen

DANCING HERON PRESS

Dancing Heron Press
Laredo, TX

www.ridingofftheedgeofthemap.com

Cover design by Robert R. Burke

Cover source photographs by Calvin Bryen

Riding off the Edge of the Map

ISBN 978-0-9674947-2-2

To my beloved family Gloria, Karis, Calvin, and Mae

Acknowledgements

Praise to the first person that put a motor between the two wheels of a bicycle. Because of the evolution of that invention I have been able to love motorcycles and everything they allow my whole life. My head still turns whenever one drives by. I owe my technical understanding of motorcycle safety to Steve Garets and the Team Oregon Motorcycle Safety Program that trained me to be a motorcycle safety instructor. Failure to apply what I learned from that program is my fault not theirs.

I want to acknowledge The Chapala Writers Group in Ajijic, Mexico for their support, perspective, and assistance in transforming me from a pedantic preacher to someone who knows better. In particular I want to thank Jim Tipton, one of the few kings of the literary world who has served as a mentor for me. Jim saw past my limited writing skill and saw the story that begged to be told. Kelly Hayes-Raitt in particular has been a delightful thorn in my side who bitch-slapped me every time my arrogance showed up and taught me how to remove the fluff and clarify what was essential in my story. Thanks as well to another member of that writing group, Mel Goldberg, who after spending a month editing my rough draft thought it best to leave it behind on an airplane to Miami. I only hope I get this book published before the flight attendant does, who found my original version in the seat back.

This book couldn't have been written if it weren't for my two riding buddies, Jake and Tom. Our motorcycle trip to Copper Canyon was an experience of a lifetime, and I am thankful every day that they included me. OK, there were times I thought we were the stupidest men on earth and I cursed the day we met, but that was only until I got home. I changed their names throughout the book not to protect the innocent but to help the guilty cover their tracks. I have and always will respect Jake's strength, determination and riding skills. I learned from him everything I know about riding in the dirt. Without his vision this ride never could have happened.

Margaret Van Every deserves more thanks than I have words to convey for her editing skills and patience with my literary naivety. Her tireless and loving efforts on my behalf astonish me. Sometimes we'd wrangle for days to refine an idea and I grew to love those wrestling matches. The result was a better book than I could ever have written without her.

I love the cover art! I want to thank Bob Burke who designed the cover and formatted the book. I appreciate his skill in capturing the layered concepts I tried to elucidate throughout the book.

Finally I offer my deepest thanks to Gloria, my wife of 38 years. She was unfailing in her support, astute in her critiques, and with a large enough personality to hold the creative space open while my story unfolded. She was beside me step by step in the hard times of living through theft, pain, frustrations and endless rewrites and rereads. I cannot thank her enough for all the psychological processing we went through to make the telling of this adventure something we can both be proud of. She never tired of me even when I was ready to give up on myself.

••

Foreword

Many years ago, a beautiful Native American maiden appeared to me in a life-changing dream and asked, "Do you want to know the secret to your life?"

"Yes, yes of course," I answered.

She stretched a single strand from a spider web across a delicate wooden hoop, carefully dividing the circle into two equal parts. "This is fire," she pointed to the left side, "and that is water," she pointed to the right side. "There is a thin space between that is neither fire nor water. That is where you must live your life!"

Since that moment, I've tried to heed her counsel. What follows is a true story of two canyons, two maps, two motorcycle journeys, and the thin space between the tangible requirements of the outer world and the Siren's call to all things interior.

David Bryen

••

Contents

Acknowledgements viii

The Real Motorcycle.. 1

What Lies Beneath 5

It's About Time 11

Frayed Ends, Loose Wires, and Raw Nerves........................... 22

Outside, Inside, Outside 37

The Call of the Heron 51

The Confession 63

The Trouble with Maps... 69

Abandon Hope, All Ye Who Enter Here 75

Life at the Ledge... 87

Under the Mud 94

What Really Broke 103

Don't Drink the Water!... 112

More or Less Moral-less in Morelos....................................... 123

The Price of Salvation 135

Beauty That Steals the Mind 139

Judge the Moth by the Beauty of the Candle 147

The Real Way Out... 157

You Had to Be There 166

I Am as Bad as I Think I Am 172

The Mordida... 184

The Water Seeks the Thirsty 193

Epilogue 198

I long ago lost a hound, a bay horse, and a turtledove, and am still on their trail. Many are the travelers I have spoken to concerning them, describing their tracks and what calls they answered to. I have met one or two who had heard the hound, and the tramp of the horse, and even seen the dove disappear behind a cloud, and they seemed as anxious to recover them as if they had lost them themselves.

—Henry David Thoreau

To find out what is truly individual in ourselves, profound reflection is needed; and suddenly we realize how uncommonly difficult is the discovery of individuality.

—C.G. Jung

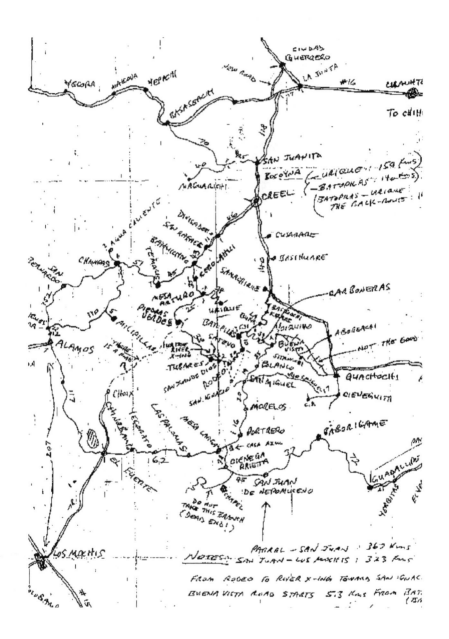

This Map is Not the Territory

The Real Motorcycle

The real cycle you're working on is a cycle called yourself.

—Robert Persig

Dante wrote, "Midway in the journey of my life I found myself in a Dark Wood." I wasn't so lucky. Midway in the journey of my life I found myself underneath my crashed motorcycle. Searing pain from what must have been broken ribs refused to let me use any muscle to push her off. There should have been a way to get out of this mess. There should have been a well of resolve somewhere and a bucket of adrenalin but they were someplace I couldn't reach. Icy hot spears radiated from my torso and shot through my body. From underneath my Suzuki I watched the rear wheel spin as the engine idled as if nothing was wrong.

It hurt to breathe. It even hurt to think, but my fear that the tank might explode with me underneath jolted me out of my desire to wait until my two riding buddies got there to help me out. They were out of sight. I managed to reach the shutoff switch on the handlebar so the engine could no longer spark off an explosion. Before I attempted to extricate myself, I did a quick survey of the rest of my body. My leg wasn't broken and my arms, although they were sore, weren't visibly damaged. I had no major contusions and my head was still attached, even though it had snapped backward when I hit the ground. I couldn't see through my helmet's visor because it was covered with fine white dust when I crashed face first into the ground.

All I really wanted to do was lie there, close my eyes, and go to sleep. "I can't go on! I'm finished!" I muttered to myself, grinding my teeth as if that would diminish the hurt.

Two sides of my brain finally came into sync. They had been in disagreement for two days, torn between the fear of abandoning my friends and returning alone to El Fuerte and the fear of continuing with them and disregarding my premonition of disaster. I had to get off this motorcycle and find my way out. I no longer cared about my once precious Suzuki. I'd just as soon kick it down one of the precipitous slopes in this stunningly beautiful area. We'd ridden two days into Mexico's wildest country, trying to get to the legendary vistas of Copper Canyon (Barrancas del Cobre) on "roads" traveled only by indigenous Tarahumara and local Mexicans scratching a living from the occasional farms. The only vehicles in there were big honking 4x4 pickups on aggressively knobby off-road tires. We'd seen only ten or fifteen vehicles all day. This was supposed to be a relaxed motorcycle tour to the beauty of Mexico's heart. These roads had already taught me more about terror than I ever wanted to know.

Even as I lay there underneath my smashed bike waiting for my two riding partners, I shook my head in disbelief and began to think about the mistakes we'd made that resulted in broken ribs, a two day ride from medical services, on nearly inaccessible roads, in territory crawling with violent drug traffickers, and in a country whose language I'd only begun to learn. We'd been lost for two days, had no way of knowing how to get where we wanted to go, kept thinking that the roads had to get better, and were too frightened to go back over the rocks, rivers, canyons, mud, and mountains we had crossed coming in. We were mentally exhausted from comparing the hand-drawn map we trusted to the brutal and uncharted countryside we'd been trying to pass through. I'd already cursed the man who had given us this hand-drawn "map" but hadn't faced our inanity for having turned this piece of paper into our Bible.

Tom, one of my fellow riders, rode on a gimpy tire with a rudimentary patch job we weren't sure would hold air. His saddlebag bracket had broken miles back and the right saddlebag now bounced like a bobble head on top of his other gear. His brakes were malfunctioning, his brake pedal and shift levers pretzel-twisted from his crashes, and his hip replacement ached. Jake, the third and strongest rider on our trip, had almost worn out his patience helping Tom and me pick up our bikes after the many times we dumped them. I didn't want to be here! Any pleasure in riding had vanished long ago. I only wanted to survive and get out. We were scared, exhausted, disoriented, hungry, out of water, and now this!

Mexico's *Barrancas del Cobre* was our goal. At the point of my wreck, we had no idea that we were at least a two-day ride from the dramatic vistas that inspired our trip. We were riding in the foothills of this massive geological marvel, traveling upward from sea level to the Canyon's 8,000-foot lip. We'd been zigzagging over, under, around, and through the southernmost river in the largest canyon system in North America. Americans and Canadians refer to it as "Copper Canyon," which is as inaccurate as staring at one of the peaks in Montana and saying, "this is THE Rocky Mountain." Six major river systems have cut their way through the basalt and granite that drain the high desert of North Central Mexico into the Sea of Cortez. The best vista is at Divisadero, where visitors can see the confluence where all the rivers join to become Rio Fuerte, or the Strong River. The name Copper Canyon comes from the deep copper color of its cliffs. The *Barrancas* are extremely rugged and cover some 25,000 square miles, more than four times the area and 1,700 feet deeper that Arizona's Grand Canyon. Because it is sparsely populated by the Tarahumara Indians, Mexico's notorious drug cartels have free reign there.

Its inexpressible beauty drew me like a signal fire on a hill, planted a buzz in my mind, and demanded that someday I find my way to bathe in its magnificence and experience the eons of geological history that are visible here. Assailed by its grandeur, I was also blinded to its treachery.

The mistakes that I contemplated while waiting for Jake and Tom happened not because I was jerked around by a wild hair up my backside and threw all caution out the side of my helmet, but from a series of what seemed like rational decisions that gradually split the world open to reveal a chasm that had no bottom. How could I, a sensible and safe motorcyclist, find myself in a situation I would never in my right mind have chosen?

The three of us had envisioned a safe and sane vista-filled motorcycle trip, not a hair-raising adventure on barely discernible roads a bazillion miles from nowhere, where for two days we'd ridden in abject fear, tottering on the edge of roads with 1,000-foot sheer drop-offs, facing the perils of water hazards, and risking our lives at the hands of drug traffickers. I had to figure out how we ended up making such disastrous decisions that took me so far afield from the reasonable motorcycling that has been a central love of my life.

I've always enjoyed the thrill of speed and acceleration but have carefully balanced my pursuit of the full life with keeping myself safe. Apart from impulsive adolescent adventures, I have avoided situations of real danger. I rode my motorcycles hard and fast but rarely took serious risks. Now, lying underneath a crunched bike, I regretted not having met this situation sensibly. We never should have been on these roads with dual sport motorcycles that were meagerly equipped for off-road riding. Two of us had no physical or mental training for the aggressive riding style such roads demanded, and we were in constant danger of being tossed over a cliff by an error in judgment, a misapplied brake, or a muddy puddle that would throw us out of control. We should have been on lightweight off-road bikes that weighed 300 pounds rather than on behemoth bikes weighing 600 pounds.

I'd spent my whole life riding on normal roads, using viable maps, and I ended up struggling to survive on an ugly, gritty, rutted, and boulder-filled excuse for a road.

••

What Lies Beneath

Let yourself be silently drawn by the strange pull of what you really love.
— Rumi

Motorcyclists love to ride. They don't really have a choice when the gotta-have-a motorcycle virus strikes. Dante said when he first laid eyes on Beatrice, "Here is a deity, stronger than I, who in coming will rule over me." Many have experienced such a moment, when the heavens open and something breaks into the soul that is more powerful than anything that has come before. Musicians, artists, luminaries, and lovers of all kinds have felt touched by something far beyond what can only be described as sacred. I felt that way about motorcycles for as long as I can remember. I didn't choose to swoon over motorcycles; that love found me and pulled me as surely as the ocean draws all rivers to itself.

Most motorcyclists are driven by this same love, sucked into its vortex, and carried along its course ever since. My older brother Jim and I have always been bound by this love. While we naively think we make the choices that shape our lives, it's more accurate to say that these passions find us, move in, and steer us. While not everyone wants to throw their leg across a motorcycle, the longing for the freedom and connection to the elements of nature is a nearly universal yearning for men and women.

To understand how I ended up with my motorcycle on top of me, I have to go back to two early and distinct events that turned me upside down. The first was the death of my mother when I was four. The second was the death of my father eleven years later. The way I compensated for these huge loses bears directly on why the motorcycle and I have been in love for my whole life, and why I was now in pain under my bike in the middle of nowhere.

We were a poor preacher's family serving an equally poor farm community in Wyoming. My mother was one of two people in the entire state to die in the polio epidemic in 1952. Mom had given birth to twin baby girls, six weeks before she died. I was four, Jim was five, and I had two older sisters. We never got over Mom's death, and how my father handled it created a breeding ground for serious emotional damage.

Her death made Dad crazy. Before he converted to Christianity he was a gang-banger, a punk kid who cruised the streets of Philadelphia looking for trouble. He loved to fight. He never lost his love for violence and when he converted and became a preacher, his new enemy became the Devil. He preached like a prize fighter in a boxing ring, cornering his prey, setting up the final flurry of punches, and knocking the poor Devil out. But he was more afraid of fear than anything else and he could not tolerate any sign of weakness or fright from his kids. Any expression of sadness or lack of control would send him into near psychotic rages. He'd fly into hysteria, whip off his belt, clench his fist and threaten, "Stop crying or I'll give you something to cry about!"

At one point he packed up my older sisters and their belongings and drove them to the steps of an orphanage because they could not stop crying. I hid my sadness and bewilderment because I was afraid that he'd deck me for showing any sorrow about Mom. I lived determined never to acknowledge any fear that would push him over the edge.

My father never got over his grief. When Mom died, Dad didn't have the emotional wherewithal to deal with his loss. He dealt with his emotional collapse by immediately courting the church's stunning new young organist who had been hired to replace Mom. His hellfire and damnation diatribes made the parishioners tremble as if they were dangling by a thread over the fires of hell. All the fear and guilt he'd pounded down people's throats came back to him as the congregation turned against him for his scandalous courtship. They went ballistic when they learned that Dad proposed to his new love and she said, "Walt, I will marry you, but only if I don't have to raise the twins." He caved in to her demands and gave my twin sisters to my aunt to raise. In private he spoke often of how that decision broke his heart.

The congregation was livid, not only with Dad, but also with my soon-to-be stepmother whose cold-hearted rejection of the twins broke up our family.

At their wedding, standing on the church steps as the rice pelted down from the bitter women of the community, I wailed inconsolably, "But they're trying to hurt Mom and Dad."

"Don't be silly, Davie. We love your new mom and your dad." I knew differently. Within a year they ran him out of town for his scandalous behavior. We were outcasts and I couldn't separate myself from the shame of their public stoning. Those early years were chaos for my brother and sisters. We'd lost not only our mother but our baby sisters as well. We'd also lost any assurance that we'd be safe and protected. Our stepmother's charms had beguiled our father in his loneliness and she had proven she had the power to turn his heart away from his own children. We children felt a sort of survivor's guilt that our twin sisters lived in a no-man's land between our family life and theirs with my aunt and uncle, but we were also afraid to complain lest Dad would explode and farm us out. I loved and feared Dad but mostly longed for his attention. He never had enough to give.

From the beginning I desperately wanted to be loved by my new stepmom, but it wasn't long before her lack of love for us showed up. She tried to erase our love for Mom and wouldn't even let us see any photos of her. She was compelled to prove that she was the better mother and tried to corral the hooligan energy of my brother and me to redeem herself in the eyes of the congregation. To "catch you boys in everything" became her lifelong priority. I adopted a paranoid habit of always looking over my shoulder to make sure she'd never catch me. Although I donned the persona of a highly religious kid, inside I seethed with resentment.

I had nowhere to turn for comfort. Dad's only idea of comfort came when he'd say, "Maybe some day our ship will come in." My inner world was a whirlwind. I learned to strap on a bold mask that hid my terror. I longed to feel at home but dared not trust anyone because I knew there was no real support. All my grief, confusion, and fundamentalist guilt put me in a cage that had no lock or key. I ached for something I couldn't put my finger on so I created a rich fantasy life and began to obsessively imagine that some day I'd come home and find a motorcycle sitting in my front yard. I lived daily with that imaginary hope. No one taught me to get what I wanted by planning and saving. I just let my fantasy sustain me.

Eight years after my mother died, the stress of my father's grief, guilt for giving up his baby girls, a failed business, and too many servings of calorie-rich potatoes and gravy took its toll. His physical heart began to reflect the emotional reality of his clogged and broken heart. After several heart attacks he was advised by his doctor to move to a lower elevation so his ailing heart might find some relief. In the summer of 1963 he accepted a new job at a church on the Oregon coast. We left the barren desert of central Wyoming and headed off to a new adventure in the land of perpetual green.

Two weeks after we had moved to Oregon, Dad shipped me back to Montana to work on my aunt and uncle's ranch. I was glad to return to my emotional home in the Madison Valley, which was only an hour away from Yellowstone National Park. I looked forward to being Uncle Noah's right-hand man, spending the whole summer with my twin sisters and fishing the Madison River. At fifteen, I had my own 1951 Dodge sedan to tear around in, tractors to drive, and quality time with my aunt and uncle. He was a mechanical wizard, who by example taught me the basic mechanical problem-solving skills that have served me so well in later life.

One morning the phone rang and my aunt screamed, "Oh no!" and burst into tears.

Before she could break out of her tears to speak, I asked, "Is it Grandma?"

She dropped her eyes and with uncontrollable sobs managed, "No, it's your father! He died this morning of a heart attack."

I spent the rest of the day crying. I was terrified of what would become of our family with Dad gone. I had no hope that my stepmom would be strong enough to hold our family together. My aunt must have read my mind, "Don't worry, Davie, I won't let her abandon you. I will finish raising you and your brother. You will always have my love!" The next morning we got on a Greyhound bus for the two-day trip to the Oregon coast.

Because I'd left Oregon almost as soon as we'd moved there, and I'd been gone for the entire summer, I walked into an unfamiliar house in an unfamiliar neighborhood, wanting to be held and comforted by something familiar, but there was no warmth there, just awkward stares from my family who had no clue what to do. We'd been trained well. Our Baptist theology left us no outlet for emotion. My stepmom said, "God took him home. He's now with Jesus." That was all. We stood around in tongue-tied silence, breathing the rancid air of grief, wanting, but not finding anything to help.

My brother Jim, however, was dancing from one foot to the other like he was standing in hot ashes. He had a sparkle in his eye that didn't fit the occasion. The rest of the family seemed to share his excitement. He couldn't hold his secret any longer. He finally broke the thick silence, "I gotta show you something."

He took me outside and made me stand in front of the garage. "Close your eyes." With my eyes closed, I heard the heavy door slide open. "OK, open them."

In the middle of a rotted-out termite-ridden wooden floor, proudly balancing on its center stand was a bright red, spanking clean, brand new Honda 55 motorcycle! I looked at Jim, open-mouthed in wonder. I'd never been so close to an actual motorcycle. I stammered, "Whose is it? Could I sit on it? How fast does it go?"

"It's ours! Dad bought it just a few days before he died."

It was all I'd ever hoped for but never expected from this impoverished family. Now sitting in our garage, right here in front of me was everything that had fueled my fantasies for years. I couldn't believe it.

"When can we go on the first ride? Teach me to ride it? What are we waiting for? Is it really ours?"

My ship had come in! It was an absolute surprise. The motorcycle had 239 miles on it! "It's ours!" Jim grinned, "We can ride it whenever we want!"

In anticipation of this moment Jim had strapped a square red and white boat cushion on the luggage rack behind the driver's seat. We jumped on and he took me for the first motorcycle ride of my life.

"Don't lean when I take a corner! Just sit there and let me do the steering! Don't wiggle so much!"

Clinging to my older brother from behind, I let him protect me from the wind. We rode and rode and rode that day all over the southern Oregon coast. The tears that flowed from the corners of our eyes were a combination of what the wind created, our grief, and our joy.

Later that day we all went to the funeral home to pay our last respects to Dad. I'd never touched a dead body before and I cringed when I warily reached across the great divide between the living and the dead and put my hand on his cold and waxy forehead. My instinctive withdrawal and repulsion contrasted sharply with the passionate buzz in my heart. I could hardly wait to learn how to ride my father's last gift.

••

It's About Time

Do you have the patience to wait until the mud settles and the water clears? Can you remain unmoving until the right action arises by itself?
— Tao Te Ching

If your mind is truly, profoundly stuck, then it might be much better off than when it was loaded with ideas.
— Robert Persig

One day fifteen years ago, after I'd ridden motorcycles for more than thirty-five years, I was loafing down the freeway on my 1,000-pound Honda Gold Wing. The cruise control was on and I took both hands off the handlebars and leaned out over the left side of the bike to see how quickly the bike would turn. I thought that leaning my weight would cause the bike to turn to the left. It took about a quarter of a mile for the bike to wander from the right lane to the shoulder of the left lane. Curious to understand why it took so long, I moved back to the middle of the freeway and gently pressed the left handlebar forward with one finger, thinking that the bike would turn to the right, but the heavy touring bike immediately darted to the left, *the opposite direction* I thought it would go. Pressing the right handlebar forward (steering to the left) made the bike immediately swerve to the *right!* Its movement was far quicker than I had imagined possible.

Holy Moly! Like Copernicus when he discovered the heliocentric universe, I realized that the bike did the opposite of what my idea said it would! I later learned that motorcyclists call this "countersteering." In short, it means to turn a motorcycle to the left you steer to the right. When I realized I'd been riding on false assumptions my whole life, I took a motorcycle training class and learned that most of my motorcycle friends were riding as uninformed and unsafely as I was. I was so impressed with what I'd learned that as soon as the class was over I decided the best way to become a better rider would be to train to become an instructor for the Team Oregon Motorcycle Safety Program. I could then offer something back to the motorcycle community.

That one revelation marked the beginning of huge paradigm shifts. Not only did many of my previous theories about motorcycle riding collapse, but many other assumptions about human behavior disintegrated as well. I began to seriously examine my own thinking processes. I became aware of the now questionable maps I'd used to negotiate life and the many stories I'd created to understand the way of the world. I'd spent my whole career as a depth-oriented psychotherapist helping others sift through their emotional histories but this new interior shift made me take a step back to better explore how humans create their views of the world.

Whereas the focus of my practice had been to help clients access feeling states, it now became important to understand how human behavior, emotional reactions, and decisions that didn't make sense to me stemmed from internal roadmaps that had taken over and fallen out of personal awareness; we live from the *ideas* or *stories* in our heads and rarely from actual data available to our senses. It became clearer and clearer to me that emotions are dependent on what goes on in the theater of the mind. I wondered how often, as in my mistaken idea of what made a motorcycle turn, these hidden stories made people experience aspects of reality that aren't there. Riding a motorcycle safely demands that riders rethink and retrain their thoughts so they can respond to hazards based on accurate physical data, not on mere assumptions of how a motorcycle stops and turns. The counterintuitive aspects of life and motorcycle riding fascinated me.

When I discovered countersteering I realized how the journey of life is more like riding a motorcycle than driving a car. Motorcycle riding represents the inner urge to become an individual, to ride in the raw open air without the metal cocoon of a car or the restrictions of culture. Every corner, every change in temperature, every smell becomes another opportunity to intimately touch our surroundings. The soul thrives when it steps away from the habitual because in the unknown it discovers itself. Life in its richest moments is lived countersteering.

My passion for discovery made my profession as a psychotherapist most enjoyable for me. Just as I always tore mechanical devices apart to understand what made them work, I wanted to know what drove relationship difficulties, what were the forces that shaped incomprehensible behaviors, obsessions, rages, or mood swings. Why was there so much difference among people and their expectations and disappointments? What made people click and what could I do to free people from the useless patterns of belief underpinning hatred, war, and mental illness? In our increasingly divisive political climate, how can people look at the same data and defend opposing viewpoints with their lives?

As retirement age began to approach, Gloria and I decided to countersteer our lives and turn toward a move to Mexico. We took an exploratory vacation to Lake Chapala and after spending less than a week there decided to buy a vacant lot and began to design a house. Moving there would allow me to do what I'd long wanted to do, ride and write. My new mantra became: Ride for the Soul, Write for the Soul. With my love of beauty, the motorcycle, individuation, writing, and curiosity, I crossed the Border and began to live the next chapter of my life.

But how did I end up here, under my bike, injured, scared out of my mind, and terrified that I'd never make it back to civilization?

When I first heard the bellow from someone in the neighborhood attempting to start up a beast, I walked towards the commotion. "What in the world do you have there?" I asked this stranger as he bent over his motorcycle. I was drawn to the earth-thumping cough of the monstrous custom motorcycle the same way bugs circle a street light at night. The rumble of the motor had pulled me out of my newly built house. "Hi, I'm

David, this is my wife Gloria." I offered my hand, unafraid of the grease on his.

"I'm Jake." A jumper cable from his car was hooked up like an umbilical cord to this monster.

I gladly offered to help, "OK, you adjust the carburetor and when it starts, I'll unhook the cables."

He nodded and we dropped into an immediate brotherhood. Every now and then the reluctant motor would explode like thunder for a few seconds, suggesting power galore. When it finally roared to life, the enormity of the engine's bellow from the megaphone pipes nearly ripped the plaster off the walls of the nearby homes. Finally it settled down into the characteristic staccato of a Harley Davidson.

"Whoa!" escaped from my throat.

The motor was a Harley Davidson, but the bike's frame was oversized and the paint and chrome were not typical of the show-off kind of chromed-out chopper rich guys parade. This cycle was all business. "It sounds like it's putting out some serious horsepower!"

"Yeah, I built this myself."

"You built it or you had it built?"

"No, did it all myself. I had a company build the motor but I designed and built the frame. It has horsepower coming out the ass."

"No shit!"

Motorcycling has a language all its own and we soon found ourselves like two fishermen swapping lies and stories about the center of our lives. "Why don't you and your wife come over and have a drink? We don't have furniture yet, but we have beer."

"We'll be right over."

They were in the process of building their own home up the street and were temporarily renting a house just a few doors down from ours. After he put his bike away, Jake and Susan came down and we all sat on our $7.00 gray plastic garden chairs in our recently finished, unfurnished house. We spent the next three hours fish-storying our exploits, focusing on touring times on our Honda Gold Wings, brushes with the law and flirts with danger, but mostly sharing familiar motorcycle lore.

Jake was unique. Could he spin a yarn! He was not only full of stories and adventures, but the way he told them seemed to increase his physical stature. His voice was strong, his body chiseled, and confidence oozed from the way he sat. He was a man who exuded the mystery, the darkness, and the danger he'd lived. I wondered about his enigmatic background and was curious to learn how and where his life had taken him. He had worked and lived in sixteen different countries as a highly recruited mechanical engineer. His personality, like his motorcycle, was dominant and I had to work hard to keep from being totally overrun by his powerful persona. There was no way I could match the number and intensity of his adventures.

"I counted once," his jaw lifted with pride, "and I've owned more than fifty motorcycles. If I saw a bike that I wanted, I bought it. It bums me out that I can't bring all of them to Mexico." Over the course of his thirty-five years of riding, hundreds of thousands of miles passed beneath his two tires. I never had the resources to buy as many bikes as I wanted and my responsibilities to my client caseload and my family never allowed me to ride nearly as much as I would have liked. Jake, a true connoisseur of everything automotive never left a car or cycle fantasy ungratified. His career and well-compensated intelligence allowed him much more time to tour. He had just turned fifty-two and retired in Mexico in order to enjoy the weather and year-round riding. I envied his financial resources.

Just because we so easily fell into "let's BS about bikes" didn't mean that he and I knew each other, liked each other, or established any basis to trust each other. Except for the endless entertainment of one motorcycle story after another, very little else crept into the conversation. Love bonds many different kinds of people, and our bond centered on our love for all things motorcycle. He'd ridden off-road dirt bikes, cruising bikes, touring bikes, race bikes, and dual sport bikes. I'd never met a man with more exposure to such a wide variety of motorcycle experiences and I looked forward to learning from him.

He told me a story about seeing his friend decapitated on a freeway abutment.

"What did you do? How did that affect you?" I shuddered.

"I puked my guts out. Couldn't ride for a couple days. Every time I drove by that place on the freeway, I'd get sort of squeamish!"

That set me off telling one of my horror stories of coming across a dropped motorcycle left on the side of the road a quarter mile from the ambulance loading a body covered with a white sheet. One story ignited another and he then told me of a man he didn't know who died trying to catch him on a curvy Oregon road and how weeks later he had to answer the accusations of the dead man's friends who accused him of being responsible for his death.

"I told them that I could average 120 mph on this section of highway and they wouldn't believe me. One of the hot dogs challenged me, 'Prove it.'

"We tore off and after the first few curves he couldn't keep up so I just kept going. After I got to the end of the section I stopped and waited and decided he'd gone back to his friends. Weeks later I came across the same group of riders who nearly assaulted me, blaming me for their friend's death. I told them, 'Ride your own ride, man; I am not responsible for another's safety. If you can't keep up, don't blame me!'"

Later there would be many times that I wished I'd remembered how capable he was of riding his ride without regard for others. With a certain glee he told me of marathon hours on the seat of his Gold Wing, pulling his trailer, passing cars, and laughing when they called him crazy for passing in the mountains on a blind curve. Later on he would tell me that he got his nickname "Stoneshirt" from the motorcycle gang he ran with as a youth because no matter what they did they couldn't find a heart inside his leathered and frozen chest.

I was thrilled that my new Mexico neighbor loved motorcycles and loved to motorcycle bullshit. I imagined the many rides available to us as we explored our new country. "When you guys move down here full time would you be interested in traveling with me?" Jake's question opened up the possibility that while retired I could hook up to his tailpipe and experience more of Mexico.

Gloria and I finished building our Mexican house but had to return to the United States to close our counseling and mediation practices, sell our house, and settle details before we could move there full time. This of course set me off on the pleasure of deciding which bike I would buy next. Because motorcyclists are serial lovers, I now had the opportunity to research the best bike to bring across the Border. No motorcycle holds our attention for very long. We pass through motorcycles quicker than through women. Attachment is rabid and fervent, and the motorcycle industry knows the fundamental male whorish need for everything bigger, faster, and newer. Exchanging an old bike for a new bike has far fewer consequences than chasing women, but the disease is the same. After several conversations with Jake and before I packed up and moved south, I sold my stinking fast Yamaha FJR 1300 and bought a Suzuki 650 cc V-Strom, which was much more appropriate for the dicey roads in Mexico. My new bike, unlike any I'd owned before, was designed as a dual sport adventure bike built for some light off-road/dirt use, though I intended to use it mostly on the highway.

Only a month or two after we had settled into our Mexico home, Jake hailed me on the street, "Hey Dave, a friend of mine from Canada is coming down to ride with me to Copper Canyon. Do you want to go with us?"

The images I'd seen of Copper Canyon had been tugging hard on me ever since I first saw its photos in a book. They murmured to a deep part of me like a seductive siren partially hiding behind a tree, beckoning with jeweled fingers, "Come and look at me!" I'd determined to follow that call one way or another. For me, the trip represented an opportunity to experience one of the top priorities in my retirement, to find a group of accomplished riders and travel together to explore the grandeur and mystery of my new country. I was also hopelessly naïve as to what touring in Mexico entailed. I didn't know very much about Copper Canyon either, except that I'd seen portions of it from an airplane flying back and forth to the United States. The pictures of it were as stunning as any I'd ever seen.

I didn't hesitate, "Yes, I'd love to join you. Tell me more. Who is your friend?"

"Tom lives in Alberta, Canada. That's his BMW in my garage. I sold it to him last year so he could come down here to ride whenever the urge struck him. We've been talking about doing this trip together for some time. This is on my gotta-do list. I've been planning this trip for years."

In the next month Jake and I spent more and more time together preparing the bikes for the trip and swapping more stories. Jake exuded a quality of confidence that, although exaggerated, made me feel that in battle or difficulty he would have no problem walking through anyone or anything if his life were at stake. I wasn't so sure, however, that he had any idea what sacrifice for another meant. He'd grown up hard, was part of a violent motorcycle gang in California, and still carried their colors. He'd been in more fights than he could recall and, according to him, never backed down from a confrontation. As a result of our talks, I developed a trust in him that quickly dissolved any trepidation I had about this motorcycle trip. If we came upon any danger, I figured I could hide behind his violent survival instincts.

During our few trips into Guadalajara to prepare and repair his motorcycle, our talks began to creep into the meaningful issues of life, rather than just repeating exaggerated motorcycle stories. His engineering career had kept him on the move from one city, country, and house to the next. I began to wonder if he'd ever had a true friend or if most people fed off his physical and mental toughness rather than taking the time to know him on the inside. I'd never met a man more traveled, but even then I wondered if he was a man running from something or running towards something. He was independent, like a bull rogue elephant that wouldn't fit into any mold. His restlessness suggested to me that whatever had been pulling at him, he had not yet arrived at home. Maybe I had something to offer him as well.

The day before we were to leave, I ran up to Jake's home with great anticipation to meet Tom, who had just flown in from Canada, swill a few beers and eat dinner. It was the first opportunity the three of us had to figure out our specific travel plans through Mexico. The general plan was to set forth from our location in Ajijic in the mountains of Central Mexico, drop over to the west coast, wander north, and at the coastal city of Los Mochis turn to the northeast to ride to Copper Canyon. Our idea was to mosey around the Canyon for a few days and then I would split and return home alone while they rode to a BMW rally in Idaho. Jake had indicated that maybe he'd continue on from there and ride all the way to Alaska, but his fierce commitment to getting to Alaska didn't show up until later. All Tom and I knew was that after the rally in Idaho, they would return to Ajijic. We were all in a hurry to get on the road.

Tom was my age, 62, still preparing for retirement and seriously considering buying a home on Lake Chapala to live here full time. Physically he appeared to be in good shape, with a graying crew cut, and he confidently shook my hand, looking directly into my eyes. I immediately felt comfortable with his outgoing style. My main concern was that he had been a lifelong cruiser. I had a prejudice against those who ride low-slung, heavy, chromed motorcycles made famous by Harley Davidson. Because they sit low so the riders can "cruise" with their feet out in front of them, they're notoriously slow through twisty roads. Cruisers are immensely popular because of the thumping rumble from their exhaust pipes and the outlaw persona they invite. Most motorcycle manufacturers are insanely jealous of the brand loyalty Harley Davidson enjoys. Every summer, more than a half-million Harley enthusiasts descend on a small South Dakota town for the Sturgis Motorcycle Rally.

From the hundreds of cruiser riders I'd trained, as well as my observations over years, I'd lumped cruisers into a category of riders less skilled, less interested in efficient cornering, and more concerned with their costumes and making it to the next tavern. They make up more than 50% of all motorcycle fatalities. The average age of all motorcycle fatalities is 51, and Tom's age and history of cruising put him in the statistical population most at risk.

I was quietly curious about how well he rode, how strong his resolve was, and whether or not he knew how to corner, brake safely, or negotiate the potholed roads in Mexico. Could he ride without needing a beer? Motorcycles and alcohol don't mix and I hoped our riding styles could meld together.

Shortly after we sat at Jake's table and spread a map of Mexico in front of us, Tom and I began to plan just what route we would take as we traveled north. We wanted to see as much of Mexico as possible on the way up and also allow enough time to explore the mysteries of the Canyon before we separated and I returned. He informed us, "Two years ago I flipped my car, landed on its top and broke my neck. Three years ago I had a hip replacement, so whatever we do, I won't ride on the dirt. A wreck on a motorcycle would be extremely dangerous for me! I don't do dirt!" On that, he and I agreed.

Jake meanwhile got preoccupied with his barbecue, "Go ahead. You guys plan the route. It doesn't matter to me."

"What time are we leaving tomorrow?" I asked as I left them after dinner.

"It's four hours to Barra de Navidad. We ought to get things sorted and packed by noon. Is that OK with you, Tom?" Jake asked.

"Yep."

"OK. Wheels in motion at noon!" I headed home, and like most nights before a long ride, I didn't sleep well. The next morning I was up, loaded, and raring to go. I rode to Jake's house a half-hour early. My hope for a timely departure collapsed when a garage floor littered with packs, equipment, and tents greeted me, and clothes scattered all over. I muttered to myself that the trip would never get underway. In a voice only I could hear I said, "Why does every trip of mine get delayed? There's no way we'll leave on time."

..

Frayed Ends, Loose Wires, and Raw Nerves

A crop of inextinguishable regrets. —Joseph Conrad

Three problems greeted me in the garage. First, Jake and his wife were at each other's throats trying to find the only keys for her car. "You were the last one to drive it! You already lost one set! You've left me alone without a key before! You guys aren't moving an inch until you find those keys!" Her voice snapped like a drill sergeant. Her arms were crossed locked across her chest and her voice was no nonsense. "It won't happen again!"

We all jumped to the threat and began searching. I nosed around their 6,000 square-foot house trying to locate the black hole that had swallowed the keys and was threatening our trip. I invoked St Francis, patron saint of lost things. Still no keys! I found out later that the patron saint of lost things was St. Anthony. No wonder it didn't work! Jake and Susan spent the better part of that day tearing their house apart to find them. Maybe our trip wasn't going to happen after all.

Second, in the middle of gathering necessary paperwork Tom said, "I can't find my insurance papers! Didn't insurance come when they transferred the title into my name?"

"No, as far as I know there never was any insurance on it."

Then I understood that Jake sold the BMW to Tom, but Tom never put insurance on it.

"Hey man, you're going to be screwed at the Border. You'll need it to get across the Border." Then as an afterthought Jake added, "I don't think I have any coverage on mine either. I hope we can find an insurance carrier that'll cover us on such quick notice. I'll get Susan to check it out."

Third, Tom's headlight worked, but not his running lights, and to make matters worse, as we were trying to figure that out, we discovered that his antilock brakes were malfunctioning. I walked around his motorcycle and bent down to take a closer look at his tires.

"David, you're the professional safety instructor, what do you think of those tires?"

"The front tire's OK but that rear tire has less than 1,000 miles left on it before you'll be in trouble. You have more than 1,300 miles before you get to Phoenix. When a motorcycle tire gets worn down this low the tread peels away fast, like it's being turned on a lathe. You're trusting your life to two small contact patches of rubber about the size of a cell phone. I say for sure you ought to get some new tires."

"Yeah, yeah, I know," Tom's eyes glazed over. "Fuck it, I'll buy one when we get to Phoenix."

"Hey, man, I'd rather start in Mexico with fresh rubber than trying to locate a new tire on a Mexican road in the middle of nowhere." He'd asked me but had little interest in my opinion.

I looked away and shrugged "whatever," but it didn't sit well that macho impatience trumped safety. We were new to each other and I didn't want to confront this issue because, after all, it was a judgment call and I'd always erred on the side of getting a new tire when the tread got thin. Had I known then that we'd be fording streams, crawling up boulder-strewn roads, negotiating the slimiest mud on the planet, I'd have insisted that he take the time to buy the most aggressive off-road tires he could find.

It quickly became apparent that there was no way to get all this done before our planned departure. Besides, we still hadn't found the missing set of keys. I suggested, "Let's call the BMW repair shop in Guadalajara and ask an employee how to activate the antilock brakes so we don't have to drive all the way in to have him tell us what to do. Maybe the keys will magically reappear."

Tom was too impatient or frightened or uncomfortable trying to communicate with a Spanish-speaking mechanic, so we decided to ride into Guadalajara to get it fixed. Somewhere in the vague recesses of my mind I remembered reading that there was a quirky solution to the intermittent ABS on a BMW, but the male allergy to slowing down in order to problem solve killed my option to go online to see if there was an easy solution.

Jake finally made the call, "We'll just have to postpone our departure until tomorrow. Let's drive into Guad to get the bike squared away before we leave."

Frustrated, I drove back to my house, unpacked my bike, and we all took off to the dealership 40 miles away.

The tension this delay created was palpable. Jake and I'd been like race horses at the gate waiting for Tom to arrive. The nightly thunderstorms that start like clockwork in late June had already begun, and we didn't want to get caught in the Canyon during the rainy season. We were on the edge of a very narrow window. If we didn't get out of town soon, we'd never leave.

Sometimes it's just good to ride, and being on the highway to Guadalajara would break the tension that had been building. It also would give me a chance to evaluate how well Tom could handle his bike and how well the three of us would ride together. Ironically, this was also the first time Jake and I'd been on the road together.

The mechanic told us that if the front brake lever is pulled before you moved the bike, the ABS wouldn't activate. While they were replacing the burned-out headlight I risked asking Tom one more time if he wanted to get a new tire. He declined again. In the meantime Susan got online to find insurance for Tom's $11,000 BMW and Jake's $20,000 BMW. When we returned from the dealership with Tom's bike working just fine, Jake's wife informed us that they couldn't get insurance until 9:00 the next morning. She also reminded us that no bikes would leave until her keys were found.

Still wondering if we would leave at all, I got a call that evening, "Found the damn keys in my luggage. See you in the morning!" At 8:30 a.m. they roared into my carport, loaded up and wearing all their riding gear. Jake wore a bright blue mesh jacket and matching armored pants and blue helmet. Tom wore a black mesh jacket and textile riding pants. I had a fluorescent green jacket and leather riding pants.

"Good morning. That was quick. You must've secured your insurance online?"

"Na, fuck em. We'll just work it out at the Border. Let's go!"

"You don't have insurance?" It didn't make sense to me to let a matter like that slide, but I didn't want to be delayed any longer either. Later Jake's wife told me that they wouldn't wait for one more hour in order for the paperwork to clear. "Na, fuck it" became a sad mantra for the rest of our trip.

Once we hit the road, our pace was fast but we were no longer in a hurry. We'd successfully dissolved the self inflicted paranoia that seemed to imply if we didn't leave precisely at 8:30, some sinister force would suck us back into the doldrums and we'd never ever escape the clutches of our gated community. We cleared the city limits of Ajijic and I pulled alongside Jake and we both stood up on our pegs, pumping our fists, "We're on our way!"

The necessity to be in motion even if traveling in a wrong direction would plague our whole expedition. I wondered if the tension I felt from this impatient exit was the same resignation so many women had expressed to me after they'd learned the hard way not to ask men to stop to ask for directions. To pause creates anxiety in a man's psyche that time is being wasted. Sad is the woman who asks why. The unspoken question that loomed over our departure was, "What is pushing this insistence we all felt to leave before we were prepared?"

Too often time becomes an enemy, as if to sit without doing anything or to wait until the time is right must be avoided at all costs. For men, moving through the world or doing some activity seems to be the antidote for the anxiety "dead time" creates. Perhaps the male psyche is allergic to stillness or maybe even allergic to the passage of time, but certainly the aversion to wasting time began to drop a fog of doom across the bow of this ship we sailed on.

Later relaxing during lunch Jake admitted, "Every year I plan a big trip on the motorcycle. Last year I had to cancel my trip because I burned myself very badly when a paint can exploded in a burn pile." He showed us the still red scars on his arms. "I couldn't go the year before because I had a stroke and didn't recover in time. Damned if I was going to let anything happen to keep me from making this trip!"

Knowing how I'm inclined to deny my needs in order to "get there" or push on to the next town before stopping for the night, I was surprised how easily Jake and Tom agreed to stop in mid-afternoon to spend the night in the quiet beach town of Barra de Navidad. For me the urge to get *there* would typically cause me to ride farther than was comfortable, but for them just being on the road was more important. Once we left the shore, a current pulled at us that made us ride hard, but getting there didn't seem to matter just then. We had stepped outside the constriction of ordinary home life and were free to spontaneously stop whenever we wanted. I liked Tom and Jake's relaxed style. Maybe I could let go of my stubborn insistence to press to my destination regardless of how much my body resisted.

However, in our relax-on-the-beach mode, another more ominous division began to appear. The beers we downed by the pool loosened our tongues and soon, common civility dissolved and we began to discuss *things*.

We started to talk politics. Rather, Tom began to tell Jake and me The Way It Is! An obdurate right wing conservative from Canada got on his high horse and belligerently tried to force his perspective down our throats. Jake and I not only disagreed with the content of his diatribe, but also the ugly way he belittled us, dismissed the USA, and tried to dominate the discussion.

Any friendly exchange of the kind of life experiences, motorcycle stories, and typical bullshit we'd enjoyed so far quickly ceased and his monologue reverted to his dogmatic opinions, beliefs, and incorrigible desire to convince us that his point of view was superior to ours. My style in these "discussions" is to present my perspective, state it enticingly and, like a fly fisherman offering his morsel to a fish, ply other waters if there is not a nibble. Tom, of course, was talking so fast that no time was allowed for someone else's idea. He was expressing his TRUTH. The verbal assault was too much. Jake and I rolled our eyes in derision and after Jake attempted unsuccessfully to explain his own point of view, he tried to break into Tom's diatribe. He tried at least ten times to get Tom to slow down and shut up. His voice kept escalating, "Tom, Tom, Tom!" until he was screaming.

The Mexican people, used to cacophony, walked down the street looking up at the frothing men on the balcony. There, on a small terrace one story above the street, a rift as deep as the canyon we were headed for, opened up and left me afraid that whatever else we experienced from that point on, we had reached the limit of our ability to communicate.

Shortly after I realized that Tom was nowhere near to dialogue, blinded and enamored by his own voice, I withdrew from the conversation and headed to a local store to buy some insect repellent. It didn't go wasted on me that I was repelled by Tom's toxic, opinionated venom. His beliefs were not just ideas his mind possessed, but ideas that possessed his mind. He seemed unaware that facts and opinions are not the same thing.

My life as a therapist taught me repeatedly how important it is to help individuals develop the ability to move out of the world of black and white, good and evil, light and dark. I also knew that deeply ingrained habits of thought take a long time to soften and allow an individual to live with paradox and ambiguity. A great sadness fell over me at that moment. Better for me just to enjoy the ride rather than hold myself out for significant dialogue after a day of riding.

This reinforced another drama we had had earlier in the day

when Tom ordered a beer at lunch. Preaching a little, I offered, "One request I'd like to make is that if you're going to drink, wait at least an hour before getting on the road again. Riding and alcohol don't mix."

"OK by me," Jake replied.

"No one is going to lay their fundamentalist anti-alcohol bullshit on me!" Tom snapped.

By the time we got on the road to Vallarta the next morning, I'd resigned myself to a cold journey. I feared the rest of our time together would be reflective of the icy feeling that chilled us as we went to sleep.

A riding hierarchy emerged for us as it always does on a group ride. Jake, the strongest rider and the one most familiar with this part of Mexico, took the lead most of the time. I'd tuck in behind him and together we'd drive the corners hard and fast. We would routinely run ahead of Tom on the curvy sections and then he'd catch up to us on the straights. Just like the night before, Jake and I stuck together. I remembered driving on this section of road years before when my wife and I were on a cruise to Mexico and we took a bus tour into the same area. I fell in love with Mexico then, and now, a few years later, to find myself pushing hard through the corners on my bike was as nearly perfect as I could imagine.

About 30 miles from Puerto Vallarta, Tom signaled us over to the side of the road, "I'm running low on fuel. We gotta take it easy."

"OK, why don't you run in front and set the pace." I thought he'd drive more conservatively to make it to the next gas station. Instead, he rode harder than ever into the corners and accelerated hard coming out. We had no trouble keeping up and the three of us rode in a tight formation, sweeping through the well-constructed roads and properly banked corners in the verdant tropical rain forest. Tom seemed to get caught up in the pack mentality and the group mind overrode his need to drive sensibly to conserve fuel. It didn't make sense to me that

Tom was driving so fast while he was low on fuel. Five miles outside of Puerto Vallarta on a very narrow and twisty section, Tom slowed, coasting to a stop on a blind corner. He'd run out of gas.

Jake volunteered to go ahead into PV to find some gas. Tom and I sat by the road, dripping wet in the humidity, looking out at the brilliant blue Pacific Ocean through gaps in the stunning tropical rainforest as we waited for Jake to return with fuel. I wanted to find common ground after the fight of the day before. We talked about our riding styles. I asked him, "You were really riding hard the last 20 miles. Why did you push so hard, knowing you were low on fuel?"

"I am not as good as you guys in the corners and with you on my ass didn't want to hold you back!"

"Oh, I didn't want to pressure you, I just love tucking in behind another rider and polishing my cornering technique. For me it's an opportunity to focus on the proper line through the corners, smooth transitions, and proper braking."

His chagrin for running out of gas seemed to soften his resistance and I sensed his desire to erase the friction between us, "Can you give me some cornering tips?"

"Sure. We taught a cornering sequence in our training classes. First, make sure you back off the throttle and do any braking *before* you enter the corner. Slow down and let the suspension settle early so you're not throwing the bike forward onto the front forks and trying to lean at the same time. By that time you have already moved to the outside of the lane and you look as far ahead as possible. Now you roll on the gas *before* you press the handlebar to initiate the turn."

"Wait, did you say to apply the throttle *before* you lean? That doesn't make sense."

"Because you want to make sure the suspension is quiet so it can work to keep the traction steady on the road. You don't want to be coasting in the corner; you want the gas back on just a smidge because when you go from coasting to gas on, there is always a jerk when the fuel injection comes on strong. That surge will upset the smoothness of the bike." I wondered if I sounded too condescending or was saying too much, but he was all ears, practicing in his mind what I was explaining.

I continued, remembering the thousand or so new riders to whom I'd explained the same thing. "You know if you apply throttle when you're leaned over in a corner, the bike jumps and bounces a bit before it settles down. If you apply what we call a gentle roll-on *before* you lean it over, all that up and down motion is gone and all the mechanical intelligence of the suspension keeps the tire's traction consistent throughout the corner."

He nodded.

"Then you press the handlebar to initiate the lean, move the bike to the inside of the corner and as soon as you see the exit of the corner, you apply all the throttle this puppy has."

Giving and accepting advice is tricky for men. It seems the Alpha Dog competition never really leaves us, and asking for help violates a primal fear of inadequacy. Fears of holding each other back, being left behind, and not being able to run with the big dogs, are other male dis-eases. This lopsided desire to win at all costs plagued not only this trip but also plagues humankind. I wanted to dive into the theory of countersteering but I'd done enough coaching for now.

In about 30 minutes, we heard the happy sound of Jake's motor rising and falling as he rode toward us. "I had to leave my camera at the gas station before they'd let me borrow a gas can," Jake said as he dismounted. "Sorry I took so long."

"Not a problem," Tom responded. "How far is it to PV?"

"It's only about five miles." We stopped for lunch in Puerto Vallarta and bounced our way through a few of the stores on the *malecón*. At lunch we asked a couple of Mexican guides for their recommendations for a good place to spend the night. One man, speaking very good English, told us that San Blas was one of the best stops for travelers going north. Eager to get on the road, we headed off.

It didn't matter to us that we missed the turnoff to San Blas and ended up in Tepic. The roads over the top of the coast range were some of the best I've ever ridden. The pace of our bikes as we danced from side to side, from apex to apex elicited sheer joy in our motorcycle souls. There are times when the motorcycle gods smile on us and give us clean asphalt, no traffic, and banked curves. Our ride that afternoon couldn't have been more spectacular. We arrived in San Blas late in the afternoon with our hearts singing.

That night we didn't have to flip a coin to see who got the bed and who got the floor like we had to the night before. In our seedy hotel in San Blas, three queen-sized beds lined the long room that overlooked the stagnant green swimming pool. We'd all endured hard times in our earlier lives and we accepted the roaches that crawled on the paint peeling walls, the lack of hot water, and the random piece of concrete that fell from the ceiling. We had all grown up poor. We looked at each other, raised our palms and said, "It's Mexico." These crusty beds held our bodies off the floor and the sheets were relatively clean. That was enough.

At 2:13 in the morning Jake and I woke with a start to Tom's incomprehensible screaming. It was like the horrifying noise of a beast bellowing for release. It sounded like a man deep in a dream stupor crying out, mumbling, unable to speak clearly, seeking to be saved from the monster that chased him. The howling kept getting louder and more insistent and discernibly more coherent. We could pick out a garbled "Jake" and something like "(inaudible).... me." I stumbled across the dark room, feeling the wall for the light switch and when the light jumped into the room, we saw Tom, stretched naked on his bed, eyes wide in fright, screaming incoherent instructions.

We hollered back, "Tom! Wake up. You're having a dream! Wake up!" thinking that he was talking in his sleep. The light revealed a man bathed in sweat in a panic. Jake and I exchanged apprehensive glances that reflected our own fright

31

and helplessness. Spears of terror ripped through me, believing he was in the throes of a stroke.

Our fog cleared a little and we began to understand that he was begging us, "Jake, roll me. David, just roll me!" Thoroughly confused at his demand, we rolled him to his side. No sooner had we done this than he snapped back to full lucidity and in a clear strong voice said, "Thank you! Thank you!" He paused to catch his breath. "I am so embarrassed." Another set of deep breaths. "I have sleep paralysis which is a form of narcolepsy and I wake up sometimes fully awake in my mind, but my body is paralyzed and I cannot move. As soon as someone rolls me I snap out of it and return to normal. It's terrifying! I feel like I am going to die in panic! I am so embarrassed! I am sorry I didn't tell you about it before!"

"I thought you were having a stroke," Jake admitted with relief.

"Yeah, so did I, but you don't need to make an apology. I'm glad it wasn't something more serious. Are you sure you're OK?"

Panting, he sighed, "Yeah."

A gentle sense of vulnerability entered as we talked in the dark about this condition he'd inherited from his father. It took me back to my college days when I first witnessed an epileptic seizure and the embarrassment and helplessness my classmate suffered. From that point on, everyone in the class looked at him and treated him with a cool and fearful distance. For the three of us Tom's crisis set a mood of vulnerability and became a bonding moment that began to dissolve some deep divisions of the night before.

With the interesting night behind us, I woke early to see if I could fix my headlights that had begun to randomly turn off. While I fussed with fuses and tested wires in an attempt to duplicate the problem, the two of them headed off to the local store for some morning gruel. They didn't find much other than orange soda, which they tucked into their bags. I was sure they felt me as a drag on their departure, but I had a growing fear that something was beginning to go bugger in my electrics. If the lights had simply burned out, then I could have bought new ones or replaced a fuse. The randomness of their illumination bothered me. I wanted it to make right before I left or at least figure out what was wrong.

This intermittent headlight failure distracted me. I often flashed my high beams hoping to see the blue hi beam indicator on my dash. Little intrusions, like the piddling, pestering fox in a fairy tale, rub the psyche raw and produce a sore spot, as if there is nothing more important than removing that irritant. I kept hearing useless voices inside my head like: "What do you think will go next? Maybe this is something that will turn out to be ominous down the road. Better to fix it here than wait until it gets worse." My deepest concern was that this was not a superficial problem like failing wires or a short, but that something in the deeper bowels of the motorcycle's computer wizardry was beginning to foul. My most consistent catastrophic vision was breaking down when I was alone on my way back to Ajijic.

Neither Jake nor Tom had as much mechanical skill as I did. Their indifference to my consternation didn't sit well with me but, as I thought about it, it was no different than my impatience when Tom burned out a headlight. We had traipsed all over Puerto Vallarta trying to locate a BMW dealership to no avail, so I impatiently urged them to wait until Phoenix to replace it. My trouble was deeper, not as easily solved as replacing a bulb. I wanted to find my electrical short or the reason my lights worked sometimes and not others. It's ironic to me now that we were to end up driving into what would become the Heart of Darkness with Tom and me without illumination.

Of course it's way too easy to look back and see what could have been omens, but at that point, none of us interpreted our lack of illumination as a sign that something awful awaited us. We only understood our problems as mechanical glitches that should have a rational solution. Retrospection provides such a brilliant ability to see our mistakes but in reality we made the best decisions possible given our emotional state and the facts available at the moment. I have often wished there was a consistent way to listen to what might appear as intuition so that it informs the present. Instead we're left with some sort of fuzzy logic *afterward*, "If only I'd listened."

While riding a motorcycle, one must discipline the mind to not look backward, but to stay attentive in the moment. It's absolutely imperative to focus on the here and now. When we make a mistake, run wide in a corner, experience a near miss, or come across some hazard in the road, it must pass from thought immediately because the next instant requires all our concentration. A moment of inattention and boom, we're in the ditch or some other catastrophe has struck. Memory has little value while riding. Forgetting what has passed and letting go of the fantasy of what lies ahead helps the rider live in the creative potential of every single moment. The attention demanded of every moment while riding is one of the reasons that I love to ride; I can't be anywhere else.

I am also committed to understanding how the intuitive wisdom that lies beyond rationality can be drawn on to inform us when our rational mind has reached its limits. The sense of intuition I am referring to is an inner voice, a feeling of dread or doom, a hunch, or a suspicious harbinger that can never be verified or put under the scrutiny of scientific experimental methods.

For years I have thought and taught that "superstition" and "intuition" are experienced similarly in the psyche. They both seem true when we sense them. Superstition rises out of improperly thought-through belief systems that we usually apply *after* an experience to understand it. Intuition, on the other hand, is an ongoing sense of wisdom that is informed by parts of the mind that function in the unconscious. Superstition gathers various bits of information and screens out others to support an underlying belief system and has little concern with the accuracy of the worldview it justifies. Intuition, on the other hand, is an ongoing perspective from a wiser though less rational process, which whispers its advice, sometimes good, sometimes bad. When I hear people say, "I prayed for a parking place and one showed up," it drives me nuts, because the number of times they prayed for a parking place and one didn't appear never becomes part of the data they use to support their belief system.

However, many have experienced situations when they knew something intuitively was informing them. Our intuitive faculties pick up patterns and memories, provide stunning creative genius, have access to personal and collective intelligence, and maybe most importantly, give us a sense that a deeper wisdom lurks beneath our western bastions of logic and data. But just as superstition is often faulty, so intuition is equally prone to error. The skill we need as human beings is to bring this level of perception into awareness so that both the logical and the intuitive processes inform our decisions. Is it intuition or hope or fear or a fabricated story that is informing my awareness at any given moment?

I cannot count the number of times when on a motorcycle ride I have heard or felt the inside warning, "DEER" or "COPS," and I slow down, become more alert or make some other adjustment. Most often I never see a deer, so I cannot verify if indeed my "warning" truly saved me from hitting one. Often when I rode in the Cascade Mountains of Oregon, the deer alert went off in my head but I'd never see one. However, I did hit a deer on my motorcycle once. The night before, I had a dream that forcefully told me to watch out for deer, but I was in a hurry to get home and refused to slow down. The deer died a dramatic death and nearly totaled my Gold Wing but I managed to keep both tires on the road and my ass out of the ditch. Before I gathered the plastic parts that were spread for 100 yards down the road, I heard the inner voice say *I told you so*. I never know if the scenes or warnings I have in my head are pure as gold or as inconsequential as dust, but I do listen.

It's easy to look back and find some ominous markings, but when I pulled out of San Blas with a full tank of gas my growing concern clawed at my insides. Why won't my lights work?

••

Outside, Inside, Outside

Destiny itself is like a wonderful wide tapestry in which every thread is guided by an unspeakable tender hand, placed beside another thread and held and carried by a hundred others.

—Rainer Maria Rilke

Even though our bikes were loaded like Arkansas migrant workers leaving a dust bowl hell headed towards salvation in California, every time we came to a winding section of road, we'd pour on power and pick up speed in order to experience the thrill of the next curve. The heart of a motorcyclist longs for the curve and says "yes" as the body moves forward slightly on the seat and the eager senses come alive singing "for this I ride." This is especially true when the road is black with fresh pavement, the fog lines are crisp, the engineered corners are banked, and the road is clean.

Nothing is quite as satisfying to me as riding with another who really knows how to ride a motorcycle quickly through the twisties. Following Jake through tight corners brought a smile across my face. As we rode from Barra de Navidad towards Mazatlán, I hoped Tom was able to apply the coaching I'd given him earlier: SLRP-Slow first, Look through the corner, Roll on the throttle, then Press the handlebar forward.

In the curves I repeat *Outside, Inside, Outside* to myself as I move side to side across my lane. This mantra resounds like a metronome when my bike and I rhythmically move from the outside of the corner close to the white fog line then to the yellow center line and back to the fog line at the end of the corner. Like dancers who abandon themselves to the music, riders, too, relish the changing tenor of tires singing on the pavement, the rise and fall of the engine's tone and the harmony of bike, road, and body.

"Outside, Inside, Outside" has also served as a living mantra for my life. I love to bring the physical data from the outside tangible world to help unfold the mysteries of my inner life. I

pay attention to my paradoxes, my moods, my internal dia-
logues, and my dreams. After rolling my thoughts back and
forth inside, I bring my attention to the demands of the outside world which make better sense when informed by what's
inside. I try to flow back and forth between the two. Motorcycling allows me the opportunity to find myself. It helps that
winding roads always follow the contours of mountains or
valleys, immersing me in the sensuality of nature, the changes in the temperature, the smell of a pine forest or the way a
cascading stream freshens the air. All the senses intensify and
celebrate the fact that we're free. Any doldrums of life dissolve
in the harmony of rubber against the road, air against skin,
and the quickening of awareness.

We'd pushed hard that day on some roads as sweet as any
I've ever ridden on. We put nearly 300 miles on the bikes,
crisscrossing the Sierra Madres to arrive in the coastal city
of Mazatlán. We settled into our beachside hotel by 4:00 p.m.
We'd fed ourselves only at gas stops on granola bars and junk
food, so before we moved our gear into the hotel we grabbed
a sumptuous early dinner on the beach outside our hotel. The
margaritas and cold beer slid down smoothly, and the enchi-
ladas filled the space between the collapsed and over-sugared
walls of our stomachs. Perhaps it was an ominous sign that
we were so capable of riding all day, denying the elementary
necessities of proper hydration, nutrition, and rest. The late
afternoon stuffing left us relaxed in the sultry warmth of the
midsummer Mexican coast.

Bikers naturally gravitate to the beer garden to lubricate
their end-of-the-day pontifications. They have a deep-seated
compulsion to talk about the close calls, the scenery, or to bitch
about the drivers that scared the shit out of them. Telling exaggerated tales flushes away the heightened testosterone and re-
sidual side effects of overused adrenals. Fear quickens the rider
and he must find a way to relieve his psyche just like an athlete
must wash lactic acid from over-extended muscles. The more

frightening the events of the day, the more balderdash we add when we tell the stories in order to flush them. The loudest biker in the bar is usually the one who experienced the most fear.

Coming down off my ride euphoria, I told Jake and Tom my theory about why motorcyclists love to ride. "When asked, riders will give their favorite reason why they ride. Most have something to say about freedom, style, adventure, or escape, but I developed a theory that I used while teaching motorcycle safety, and I guarantee I have a better reason than anyone!"

"OK, give him a drum roll!" They pounded the table.

"Here's the ultimate reason why we ride. Most men don't know how to dance. We're afraid to move our hips. Nothing is going on in our lower parts; we're all stuck and frozen down there. But," I raised my finger for emphasis, "every time we drive into a corner and we dive down to the apex and we come up the other side; every time we crank on the power and feel the acceleration, all our blood rushes to our ass. This area that doesn't get near enough attention celebrates and cries out to be juiced again and again. It's no wonder so many men like the thunderous vibrations of a Harley because it vibrates their cock and wakes them up."

They both nodded, "Yeah, that's right. When you take a corner in a car, you get thrown against the side of the car, your head smacks the window, and you have to fight centrifugal force in every corner."

"Yep, but for us every corner's a thrill and our ass gets all the attention. It's the AADD the Ass Attention Deficit Disorder that makes us ride!"

We laughed. Jake added, "Maybe that could be a new pick-up line in a bar, 'Hey baby, be kind to me, I suffer from AADD!'"

Back in the hotel room a contrite Tom announced, "I'll sleep on the floor tonight." He hadn't mentioned running out of gas, but the embarrassment of his terrifying paralysis the night before lingered in the air. I wondered if his sleep paralysis would happen every night. His offer felt like an apology, as if trying to appease any lingering judgment Jake and I might be carrying. He had already worked on the hotel manager to negotiate a bargain price for the three of us to share a beachfront room with two queen-sized beds. Unspoken and clear we knew that we wouldn't share beds. Jake, not to be outdone by Tom's chivalry, insisted, "Naw, fuck it, I'll sleep on the floor."

I let the two of them fight this one out. I figured I'd have to take my turn at some point, but saw no real value pretending that I'd willingly offer my bony backside to the cold tile floor. I made a limp offer anyway, "Let's flip for it," hoping their competition for most macho would continue so I might never have to ever sleep on the floor.

At an impasse, they decided that there was room enough to pull the mattress off the bed. Jake won the toss and chose the mattress. Tom, the goat, had to sleep on the box springs. We could barely walk across the crowded room with all our gear clogging the floor, but no one lost face in the decision.

Tom had, however, apologized several times and acknowledged being embarrassed about his narcoleptic paralysis. I didn't want him to remind me of the vision burned into my head of him lying in bed, one bare light bulb shining on his naked sweaty body on top of the sheets in that very dirty room with plaster peeling off the 14-foot ceiling. I could have done without the memory and sick feeling in my gut when he struggled in his paralysis to tell us that all we had to do was to turn him over. I didn't want to touch his naked body glistening from his panic. Running out of gas outside of Puerto Vallarta didn't help with his self-esteem either and that is why he was so insistent on sleeping on the floor.

The three of us were outwardly polite but inwardly disturbed. We'd been on the road for only three days and had twice nearly come to blows, run out of gas once, and had the strange experience of Tom's sleep paralysis. My encounter with Tom's political fundamentalism the first night out felt too much like war to me, and a cold spot was still growing in my belly. I'd ridden all day replaying these conversations over and over, grinding my teeth and shaking my head in disgust. It's not good to ride distracted and I wanted to find ways to reach common ground so I could let my tension go. In the presence of Tom's unfettered anger I felt danger and wanted distance from him. If I could understand him, maybe my increasing judgment would go away.

Fundamentalism of any kind, others' or mine, has always frightened me. Whether political, religious, ideological, or racial, I feel that the fundamentalist unconsciously desires to kill a person who has a differing point of view. That is why we sense danger during an argument. In the presence of disagreement, commonality disappears and fierce tribal loyalty surfaces, turning the opposition into an enemy to be destroyed. I recognized this threat from growing up in the home of a Baptist preacher. Questioning an orthodox doctrine risked excommunication. I had to do so much intellectual work to extricate myself from the lopsided belief system in which one way is the only way, rules are black and white, one either spends eternity in heaven or hell, you were either for us or against us, saved or unsaved, liberal or conservative, good or bad. Pat, pithy answers, irrational formulas for living and, worst of all, the need to find enemies in power that were to blame for every problem characterized all forms of fundamentalism I'd ever run across.

Although the argument in Barra de Navidad had ended on a civil note, none of us had dared walk into that chasm of political contempt again. I was afraid our ten-day trip would get ugly if I couldn't quiet my agitation. If I continued to react to Tom's reptilian dogmatism with my own specialized and equally dismissive fight response, I would soon become more sinister, with a sophisticated form of mockery; left to simmer, my fear would turn to judgment. I would soon find his vulnerable spot and drive a verbal spike through his heart and in the end, just write him off.

My way out of these situations in the past was to figure out what had happened in a person's life to turn them rigid. Whenever I worked with clients I didn't have compassion for, my distance always dissolved when they told me their story, revealed their wound, or explained the core emotional trauma that had been shaping their psychological problem. When I had a roadmap of their life and could see where they were coming from, my judgment dropped away. I made sense out of psychological or relational difficulties by understanding that their symptoms were simply the visible scars of an unresolved wound.

While in graduate school I read something that became a core idea in my treatment of clients. The author said, "To know the myth is to know the man." That may be the single most important thought around which my life has circled. In order to understand the painful choices anyone made or what made people turn out the way they did, I had to appreciate the deep ideas and traumas that shaped their lives.

So many conflicts resolve when both parties can get below surface opinions and gather a sense of what the other person is afraid of. Understanding the path the other has traveled creates a commonality that supports rather than tries to destroy. I wanted to find out what had made Tom so strident. Maybe my judgments wouldn't sour during the rest of our trip. I wanted a spiritual connection to the Canyon. I wanted mystical stillness to break over us at sundown, to hoist a bottle of rum in ecstasy, and drink to the dark mysteries of life. I didn't like the isolation I was feeling and wanted to unzip my skin, drop my own masks, and show Tom the crap that had shaped my life.

I especially hoped that I could describe where my life took on deeper dimensions so we could have more to talk about than the superficial braggadocio of our ride. One of the most valuable lessons I learned while undoing the foundations of my own rabid one-sidedness was that people's personal psychology shapes their belief systems.

Unfinished emotional business, personal family events, and unaddressed wounds, not logic or clear thinking, cause an individual to gravitate to an inflexible philosophy or belief system. The stridency of one's convictions is in direct proportion to the size of the wound it covers. Idealistic and aggressive political or theological positions grow directly out of the fury that has been pushed out of awareness. I hoped to get under the cover of Tom's vengeful armor.

After a dip in the top floor swimming pool and another bottle of rich, dark Mexican beer, Jake went to the room to listen to music. Tom and I took an evening stroll down the malecón. He hunted for an opportunity to reengage the political discourse and spew his favorite opinion at me, but I dodged his bait and pressed to understand him more. "You told us the other night that you inherited the sleep paralysis from your dad. What was he like?"

He dropped away from his opinions and began to share his history. "My father was an immigrant from Czechoslovakia. Life there was uncommonly hard, and he came to Canada with absolutely nothing, no money or friends, and through grit and hard work, disciplined saving, and frugal living, he provided a home and education for us all." The far-off look and moistening in Tom's eyes suggested something different from anything he'd shown before. Maybe he was not as hard-crusted as he let on.

"But he was a merciless man who would harshly punish us, kick the shit out of us if we did wrong. He let me know that if I didn't like it, I was welcome to leave. He left me bruised and bloodied many times. He allowed no discussion, was always right, and enforced it with a hard and quick fist. I left home early and have been on my own since my teenage years."

I warmed more and more as I listened to the details of his history and the level of his suffering. Although his father seemed more physically brutal than mine, I wanted to share more of my own upbringing, hoping that we would find something other than riding to bind us together.

Another group of people walked up to the statue of the motorcycle we were standing by, took some pictures, rubbed it a little, and walked away. Tom continued his story. "After I left home at fifteen I lived like a wild man. I was deeply involved in drugs and alcohol and had no love life. I don't know how I made it through." He paused and his eyes retreated from the surface of the statue as he floated downwards where something quite painful was struggling to make it to the top. "I was a mess, man!" His eyes, now unfocused, looked down at the tile on the *malecón*, out to the darkening Pacific horizon and back to the ground. He inhaled and his long sigh alerted me to a coming confession. His comments about his embarrassment over the last couple of days had given us permission to be softer with each other.

I wanted to encourage him to continue by telling him some of my story, how as a kid I too had to suppress all my disagreements or get clobbered by my father's God-guided fundamentalist fist. I began to see that Tom's father was similar to mine except mine simply switched his violent temper towards heathens, Catholics, sensuality, smoking, drinking, cussing, dancing, and anything else that was fun. When he saw his kids headed for the fun things he used to do, he'd whip off his belt quicker than a rattlesnake strike and remind us while swinging the two-inch wide leather across our backsides, "This hurts me more that it hurts you." He rationalized his violence under the guise of helping us become more Christ-like.

Instead of sharing my details with Tom, I wanted him to understand that his reaction to his father's rages stemmed from the same kind of father-wound I experienced; our dads had no other way to handle their fear and helplessness and tried to control our fate through violence.

I told him, "Although on the outside I looked compliant, religious, kind, upright, and good, inside I raged against Dad's Christianity. A strong inner drive devoted to my integrity kept me stubbornly true to myself and fostered the outlaw part of me. I didn't take my battle out in the same way you did by raising hell, I battled in my mind and with my clients to get free from the debilitating beliefs that are inherent in fundamentalism. My father and I developed an intense and unhealthy rivalry because I was such a show-off. He loved being the center of attention and I learned well from a master how to draw attention to myself. He'd often say to me: 'You're too big for your britches.' I never knew what britches were but I lived in fear because he constantly threatened to knock me off my high horse.

"Tom," I went on, "you and I have found different ways to express our rage at our fathers, but in moments like this I feel that we're brothers in our desire to make it better."

We were still sitting on the stone wall next to Mazatlán's bronze statue of Pedro Infante Cruz sitting astride an ancient Harley Davidson. He was an idolized Mexican singer/actor and thousands of visitors passed by this monument weekly to be fed from and to feed his spirit. People passing by would reverently rub their hands across his features and had polished the bronze patina to a shine. Occasionally we would likewise pause in our discussion and unconsciously rub our hands across the people-polished fender of the motorcycle. We were finding old and important things to talk about. The statue helped. When other visitors walked by, we'd pause and enjoy their experience of the bronze Harley. Lightning splashed across the sky, announcing a thunderstorm as the humidity pressed down on us.

"David, you said something the other night about shame. I've been chewing on it ever since. After we had our argument in Barra, you talked about what you had come to understand about shame and how it became one of the center points of your work as a shrink."

I was surprised that our discussion had sunk in at all but was glad that it had some effect. "Shame," I'd offered that night "is the most undiagnosed psychological dynamic in Western culture. It ought to be a clinical classification but it's not."

Now Tom wanted to pick up that thread, his tone was curious, not argumentative, "You said shame was a destructive thing, right? But unless there is shame, a society cannot control its people. It seems to me you need to keep shame alive in order to make people behave. That is what my dad did."

Something else was hidden in his question as if he had his leg caught in a bear trap that he couldn't pry open.

"Shame and guilt are two close but quite different brothers. What you're talking about is a social conscience, something alive in a culture that explains the rules and the consequences when you break them. If a person develops in the right direction, care and compassion for their society replaces fear of punishment, but before that takes place, we use fear and guilt to keep people in line.

"But shame is different. Shame is a dynamic inside the head that comes to us in the voice of the inner whisperer that says, 'You are BAD because you did something that broke the rules.' It is a haunting voice that continually hammers us with this message, 'You are no good! You shouldn't exist! You're flawed! Someone is going to find out that you're a fraud. You must find a way to change and make yourself perfect.' This inner voice has recorded every flaw, failure, and shortcoming, and reminds us if we ever forget. No one teaches us how to turn it off.

"Guilt comes from the truth of your having violated something essential for self or society, but shame is a lie that says you're unworthy and keeps telling you that same dirty lie. Guilt says you did wrong, shame says you ARE wrong because you did wrong. Universally it implies that you will be abandoned. The fear of condemnation or shame is HUGE in our culture."

I paused to let him sort out the difference. Still unclear, he pushed back, "Isn't that right? Aren't you bad? Shouldn't you be punished?" His question reminded me how so many live with the idea that they're bad, unworthy, or flawed and simply get used to this feeling of internal condemnation as if they deserve to be hurt. Shame is one of those unquestioned assumptions that slides over our collective soul and operates without our conscious awareness.

"Every society provides a way for redemption, whether through physical punishment, banishment, acts of contrition, etc., after which the society welcomes the offender back guilt free and no longer in need of punishment. Shame on the other hand is a relentless, internal condemnation that pierces us to the core. When we are shamed by others, it feels like our very existence is being threatened and our reptilian protectionism snaps to attention and will immediately lead to a quickly escalating fight."

His wrestling match was not with me; he was clawing to find a clue for his own release. A light came on, "It's kind of everywhere, isn't it? It doesn't let you go!"

"Exactly! I love to use the word 'pernicious' to describe it. It's everywhere in our culture: sports, competition, war, politics, you name it. Did you ever think how advertising could be effective if they didn't use the idea that 'You are not enough, your house isn't big enough, your teeth aren't white enough… just imagine how many more women you'd attract if you smelled better, looked better, or drank the best beer!' How many women suffer from the crazy idea that their value is dependent on looking young, with huge tits and beautiful flowing hair? Advertising cannot exist as we know it without making us feel inadequate. Take shame and the fear of hell away and the church could no longer justify its existence."

He gazed over the clouds that were taking on the color of a deep purple and yellow bruise, and tried to absorb the idea that shame and capitalism go hand in hand. He finally got it, "Yeah, you're right. A new Harley with more chrome will make me a better man."

To help him see how shame operates outside of our control, I asked him, "Were you embarrassed the other night because of your sleep paralysis episode in San Blas?"

"Of course!"

"The old shame beast had a hay day with you, didn't it?"

My question made him sit back and ponder the way his own shame and embarrassment thrashed him around that day. "Yeah, I kept wondering about what you and Jake were thinking. A voice kept repeating the idea that you guys would think less of me."

I was glad that he caught the idea that he was at the mercy of this relentless voice in his head. That haunted far-off look came back on his face. He paused. A familiar pressure inside my chest alerted me that we were about to cross a significant threshold. He was readying himself to spill a secret that had been unsafe to share before. The air turned somber, the hair on the back of my neck rose, something like a shiver of wind on a cool night rattled across my awareness. The brewing thunderstorm seemed to announce the significance of what we were approaching, testing if we could be a safe harbor to protect what we'd been building.

For many, the counseling office becomes the container where the burdens of guilt and shame are unloaded and moral quandaries sorted. The search for a good therapist is a hunt for a place of safety where the dark parts of life are permitted to surface without judgment. The kind of therapy I did was full of confessions. In the course of my practice, I'd had three people confess to deaths at their hand that had gone unpunished. Each of these confessions severely challenged my sense of ethical responsibility, commitment to confidentiality, and loyalty to the trust given to me while clients worked out the guilt that wracked their lives. I'd watch their eyes as they'd silently try out their confession, wrestling with their cruel internal critic.

How the soul carries its secrets and how the secrets shape the soul are intricately bound up with shame. Shame and fear are the two elements that destroy the soul. Shamed people fear they will be shamed again so they isolate the deepest and hungriest parts of themselves from those who could offer them support. And now Tom and I, near mortal enemies of opinion the night before, were walking toward a new brink.

His confession dangled on the precipice just behind his lips. I could feel it. We headed back toward the hotel as the clouds thickened and the thunderstorm approached. Unwilling to let the growing sense of safety pass and before we dropped away from our newfound warmth, his head dropped, "I'll tell you about my sister later."

••

The Call of the Heron

What you seek is seeking you. —**Rumi**

We got back to the room just before a lightning strike wiped out the transformers and the city lights went black. Cheers erupted from the natives on the dark streets below, freeing an ancient hedonistic upwelling, and as soon as the hotel's emergency lights kicked in, we bounced down the steps to participate in the dark celebration. Only the headlights of the cars lit the streets as we jumped over puddles to the islands of candlelight under the awnings of sidewalk cafes until we found a little store illuminated enough to buy some supplies for the next day's travel. We hoped the storm would pass so we wouldn't have to ride the next day in the rain. Later we dropped off to sleep lulled by the ocean, the roll of distant thunder, the drone of the hotel's generator, and the splash of car tires on the drenched street.

The oppressive humidity passed with the storm just as the clamminess that existed between Tom and me had vanished. Tom and I rose early and headed off for breakfast together while Jake again slept in. At breakfast, after the previous evening's closeness, I wondered if Tom would continue his openness and unload his burden about his sister. I was keen to share some of my deeper stories as well.

Our conversation struggled to life like a cold engine that hadn't rubbed the sleep out of its eyes. He seemed uncomfortable yet eager, trying to find a way back to where the conversation had left off the night before. Starting on more familiar ground, he blurted, "Ya gotta be careful around Jake! Sometimes he gets a wild hair up his ass and just darts off."

"What do you mean?"

"The other morning in Puerto Vallarta when Jake cut across three lanes of traffic to get to Wal-Mart…"

"Oh, yeah, I was really pissed off! I wanted to jump down

his throat but was afraid of making a scene."

He advised me, "Jake can be a selfish bastard and not think of others sometimes, so just be careful. I've ridden with him enough to know. Give him plenty of room. What happened anyway?"

"I was in the left lane. He was even with me in the middle lane, and all of a sudden he cut hard to the right across all that traffic and then across that skinny street that paralleled the main road. When I tried to get over four lanes to follow him, that fuckin' bus with those six-inch Ben Hur knives on its lug nuts nearly clipped me and wouldn't let me in. Did you see the size of those spikes? Those bus drivers are dangerous! By the time I worked my way across the lanes, you guys had disappeared. When I finally spotted you in the parking lot I was past the exit and didn't see a way back to where you were.

"He peeled out of the parking lot to find me. To get back to the Wal-Mart parking lot we had to drive the wrong way down the exit ramp, do an illegal U-turn right in front of a traffic cop. That's why I was pissed and refused to talk while we looked for your headlight.

I didn't admit it to Tom, but I had been caught in a pouty man mood. It had concerned me to lose contact with the group. "We gotta talk about what we're going to do if we get split up! We haven't made a plan. Do you know what to do if you get lost? I don't. Are we supposed to go ahead and wait, or go back? We could get separated and mess up the whole trip! We'd be fucked."

I made a mental note that we needed to have the discussion about what we would do if we separated. It was one of those necessary parts of traveling in a group and the lack of such conversation began to spread an ominous cloud over me. We just hadn't created the atmosphere that invited such a conversation.

The heaviness of that particular episode had cleared for me but a wedge was beginning to insert itself in our group. Tom and I were talking about real things, making our own bridges but I was uneasy about the widening rift with Jake. My concerns had to do with a basic lack of cooperative decision-making. The agenda to ride seemed to miss the opportunities to enjoy what we came across. We'd sped by vistas, jumped over the *topes* at full speed, and blew past dappled sunlight in the rain forests, not because any of us were oblivious to beauty or wonder, but because the ride simply took over, and like a float in a cascading river, we were caught in its current and forced away from meaningful contact with the land around us. Unfortunately, beauty and speed seem to be in constant conflict. We hadn't developed a way to free ourselves from the allure of speed to spend time in the beauty of nature. Basking in the delights of nature seemed more like an interruption of our agenda to get wherever "there" was.

I hoped that our breakfast conversation would warm things up. I wanted the feeling of openness to pervade our trip. The mystical dimensions of my interior life whisper rather than shout, and I wanted to make sure that when we got there I could find room to thoroughly experience the richness of the Canyon instead of blasting through it. I've always had a hard time defending and protecting the tenderness at my core. I wanted to be understood. I've covered much of my life in silence, as we all do, because the subtleties of my deepest experiences are too fine for words. While I understand their significance, words are too coarse to capture the complexity of my inner feelings.

We were headed to Copper Canyon where I hoped for an expanded connection to nature. I needed to have space and time to pause so that the excitement of traveling somewhere wouldn't prevent me from arriving anywhere. When Gloria and I rode together, she could at times get me to pause at a stunning vista, but most often during such pauses, my throttle hand would twitch and urge me to get back to the road. I always thought it was ironic that the places on earth with the best vistas that invited me to stop and reflect were also surrounded by the curviest roads that, in contrast, invited me to get back on the bike and ride fast through the corners.

The inner map that guides my poetry and philosophical reflections is in conflict with the speed-loving motorcyclist. I've never quite settled just how to attend both the part of me that wants the exuberance of riding and the contemplative part that craves to sit inside beauty and absorb it. I was waiting until I arrived at the Canyon to settle into the deeper parts, hoping that what I experienced there would translate into some significant writing. I wanted to create enough room for the Poet and the Rider to come together for a while. My communication with Tom and Jake had not deepened enough for them to know how focused I was on simply sitting timeless in the grandeur of Copper Canyon. We had already proven we could easily override basic body needs and I hoped for some understanding with Tom that I was afraid I couldn't elicit from Jake.

The waiter came by to pick up our vouchers for breakfast. I hoped that the typical warm morning on a beachfront in central Mexico would continue to close the distance between Tom and me. I liked the calm time we were having. Cautious as a hand that enters a nest to retrieve eggs, I decided to open up more of my spiritual journey. I wanted Tom to become an ally. If he couldn't understand the significance of what I was about to share, I feared that the rest of the trip would be lonely.

I waded in like a swimmer entering frigid water, "I know my experiences aren't common, but I'd like to tell you about one of the most important events of my life. I'm kind of careful who I tell this story. Are you interested?"

"Yeah sure."

"It all started for me at a men's conference in 1988." His eyes were on mine and he leaned forward in his chair. "One hundred men gathered for a workshop in the mountains outside of Seattle. It was the very beginning of the Men's Movement and for several years the leaders had been running workshops awakening men to the deeper sacred masculine parts of the psyche. On the last day of the conference, Robert Bly read his 'Water' poem, and when I heard the words '...We are thirsty for the heron and the lake, the touch of the bill on the water,' something thumped my chest. I looked down, expecting to see someone's hand on my chest but no one had tapped me. I can still feel the shock from that physical sensation that didn't come from someone trying to get my attention." I firmly rapped on my breastbone so Tom could hear and feel the physicality of that bone against bone tap. Tom, mesmerized by my story, reacted just as I had, and jumped back nearly as startled as I had been.

"When I got home I wept with joy as I twirled my six-year-old son and nine-year-old daughter. I tossed them in the air, hugged them, and rolled on the floor. The vivifying energy that surrounded me was like a contagious aura that swept up our whole family, 'Daddy's home, Daddy's home!' Their celebration was more than I expected. When I tried to describe the conference to my wife, my sobs of joy kept interrupting me. I'd come home with something inside as tangible as if I'd found a brother that had been lost since birth. I wanted to dance, to sing, play the drum, and of all things, write poetry. My chest buzzed like there was a beehive inside!"

I turned my focus from that memory and directed a question to Tom, "Did you ever notice that some things become more powerful when you tell them to someone who loves you?"

"Yeah, you're right."

"It was like that for my wife and me. Like the water behind an earthen dam that had been breached, a new layer of excitement and connection broke over me and I was flooded with a sense of what I can only call sacred. A couple of weeks after I returned home from the conference, I had a vivid dream of a Great Blue Heron standing in the shallow part of a lake silhouetted against the amber peach sunset sky. Only a dream, but that dream began a series of astounding synchronicities involving Great Blue Herons."

I leaned back in my chair and took another sip of my creamed coffee. The rhythmic swoosh of the morning waves continued to relax us, and the warmth of my memories poured out.

"In the previous five years I'd spent building my lake cabin, the heron didn't make an impression on me. However, from that day on, the heron was a constant companion. I began writing poetry and the heron would fly to the top of my cabin and, like the old heralds that would blow their trumpets to announce something important, chortle its encouragement as I tried to express the buzzing expansion in my heart. Poetry gushed from me like champagne exploding from the bottle."

Tom was still with me. He hadn't even sipped from his coffee.

"Whenever I'd begin to tell others of my awakening experiences at the men's conference, the strange vibration in my chest, or of my encounters with the heron, a heron would fly by. I noticed that the journal I bought just before the men's conference had herons splashing on the cover. One day at my cabin I went to my bookcase and found Barry Lopez's poetry book *River Notes, The Dance of Herons*, which I'd never read. As I looked up from the book in my hand I saw another heron, 15 feet away out my window, looking me in the eye.

"It wasn't so much the heron's appearance itself," I tried to emphasize, "but that a heron always showed at times of significant thought, like an exclamation point to validate and fortify the awakening I was experiencing."

While I was leading up to revealing my life-changing experience with the heron, I tried to measure Tom's ability to understand what I was saying. I didn't want him to view the appearance of herons in my life as the kind the common occurrence someone has who turns his attention to something new and then sees the new object everywhere. It was important for me to demonstrate that the synchronicity between my significant thoughts and a heron's physical appearance continued to astound me. After all, the heron experience was the most dramatic thing to ever happen in my life and I didn't want to have it diminished.

"Tom, do you understand synchronicity?"

"Yeah, it's coincidence isn't it?"

"It is really more than that. Things come together all the time, but synchronicity is not just coincidence. It's a meaningful connection of two or more unrelated events that awakens the whole psyche to a realm of wonder. We live in a world of cause and effect, and are trained to think that everything we experience is caused by something else. However, synchronistic experiences have no physical cause-effect relationship. It is as if there are two parallel realities that exist side by side and sometimes they coincide and wonder breaks through. It is the amazement itself that is so astounding.

"For me, all of a sudden I realized a connection between my thoughts and physical events in the world. How could a heron know that I was sitting down to write poetry and come close and chatter to me, which only made my wide eyes open wider? I was stunned by an immediate awareness and connection to all things. A light came on for me. The common boundaries between matter and spirit, animal and human, dissolved and I experienced a oneness that altered the way I was in the world."

I wanted to lay the foundation so that Tom would see that this experience with the Great Blue Herons shattered nearly all the rules about reality that I'd lived by. Just as my discovery of countersteering pointed me to my small and inadequate understanding of motorcycle physics, my encounter with the herons completely blew away my previous understanding of cause and effect.

"For example, not too long after the herons and I started this tango, I was sitting with a dear friend visiting from Chicago who'd introduced me to the work of Carl Jung more than ten years before. Warm and relaxed, sitting on the dock, sipping a glass of Merlot, I began talking about the finer details of psychological and spiritual opening that had overtaken me and tried to get him inside the numinosity of the heron's effect on me."

Tom screwed up his face, "What's numinosity?"

"*Nuemen* is the Latin word for that which glows on its own. My encounters with the herons began to glow as if a fluorescent pen had highlighted them. They lit me up with a sort of buzz inside. Every encounter became increasingly electrified. I lived wide-eyed and stunned."

He nodded, "OK, go on. I can imagine it, but it's never happened to me. What happened next?"

"While I was reading a poem to my friend to explain the similarities between what I was coming to understand and the way a shaman works with different layers of reality, two herons landed a few yards away and to our surprise and delight began their mating dance! They mirrored each other, stretched their necks in full extension, spread their five-foot wings as wide as possible, danced from one foot to the other in the shallow water, and then in unison swayed their heads to the right and to the left just like the greetings we sometimes give each other, kissing both cheeks. They would pause with the sun shining luminous through their nearly touching, bright yellow beaks, and their breast feathers standing out erect from their bodies, and then repeat their hypnotic swaying."

He closed his eyes, his head bobbing back and forth mimicking the heron's cadence. Then as if he too could hear their same music he chuckled, "You paint good word pictures."

"*¿Más café, Señores?*" startled us out of our trancy moment. "Where are you from?" the waiter asked in perfect English. "I grew up in San Diego." He warmed up our coffee as we all small talked and he moved on to serve the next table.

"The heron dance was so beautiful!" I closed my eyes to remember not only the dance, but also the way my friend and I were spellbound.

"My encounters with herons continued until the pivotal point of my life on the 4th of July, 1988. That weekend, out of the blue, I was grabbed by a fierce compulsion to find a single heron feather. I spent three days of that long weekend scouring the entire lakeshore in my canoe, you know, like Parsifal searching for the Holy Grail. I had to have a feather!"

Epiphanies such as I was about to share with Tom have always stirred human imagination. They speak to an archetypal longing of every human being to touch and to be touched by the wild in the animal. D.H. Lawrence voices this in his great poem Snake when he reminisces about his missed opportunity to encounter a snake that had emerged from the rocks in a wall. The poet, caught by his fear picked up a stick and threw it at the snake, which slithered back into its underground home. In his regret Lawrence wrote:

> …For he seemed to me again like a king,
> like a king in exile, uncrowned in the underworld,
> now due to be crowned again.
> And so, I missed my chance with one of the lords of life.
> And I have something to expiate:
> a pettiness.

The obsession to meet an animal in the raw drives sportsmen to kill, eat, domesticate, or trophy animals. Human fascination with zoos, animal programs on TV, and circus animals, reflects this longing to explore the hidden essentiality of animals. They're like points of light in an otherwise dark landscape. Something missing in our lives is fulfilled by intimate connection with these lords of life.

Tom's falcon gaze, as he moved forward on the edge of his chair, let me know that he was fascinated by what was coming.

Looking around as if keeping a secret from casual listeners, I dropped my voice and leaned forward on my elbows, "Nearing dusk on the third day of my compulsion, I silently slipped my canoe through the mirror-calm water. I spotted a Great Blue Heron hunkered at the edge of a meadow on the lake's shore only 100 feet away. Its head down between its shoulders, its yellow needle beak and sunflower-colored eyes, focused like daggers, followed me as I approached. Breathless, I almost willed myself closer and closer. The Charcoal Mystery, 'Ole Shypoke,' as the old frontiersmen of Oregon called them, froze rather than scolded me. I froze too.

"Stunned that this beautiful bird allowed me to approach so close before it moved, I watched as it turned from me and struggled into the tall meadow grass. Its retreat invited me, almost as if it had gestured with its head, like the cloaked shadowy figure at the corner of the dark alley whispering: 'Hey fella, over here, follow me, I have something to show you.' Terrified, I dropped into my quietest place and barely breathing, rounded a tall tuft of grass and nursed my canoe to shore.

"It struggled through three-foot-tall grass and disappeared into the meadow. I paused, observed its direction, slunk down as close to the ground as possible, careful not to stand up for fear it would fly away. I guessed at the angle I should crawl that would allow me to intersect its path. I oozed out of my canoe, slid on my stomach, snaking through the soggy grass blade by blade. Parting each clump with my hands I drew myself forward with my elbows. I was pulled forward as if I had a chain around my neck. All my senses were as alert as if there were an eyeball on the end of every hair of my body, watching, listening to everything. I thought I might get closer than ever to a heron. I had no idea what I would do if I ever got there.

"Tom, what do you say when you meet a god?" I took a breather.

He could only shake his head as he tried to relate to the image I'd just made. His eyes returned to mine and he nodded for me to continue.

"I worked my fingers through one last clump, separating the grass, and inched forward." I put my chin close to the table and pushed my plate and coffee cup aside just as I had when I parted the grass. "And there, with its beak only inches away from my eyes, a Great Blue Heron filled my entire field of vision."

I gestured to Tom with my hand six inches from my face. "Right here. It was this close! It had collapsed on its belly and just stared at me!"

"God!" escaped through Tom's drawn breath.

"Now, what was I supposed to do? I don't know how long we lay there transfixed, eye-to-eye, my blue eyes peering into the yellow ones that were boring a hole all the way to my soul. This majestic stalker and I, my nose almost touching its stiletto beak, were knitted together by forces new to me."

"What'd you do? My God!"

"I had no idea what to do next so I waited. Tom, how can I explain that the veil that once separated animal and human was now nothing more than a tattered remnant? I didn't blink! Should I stay, retreat in reverence, or pray? I knew I'd been called to this moment. Never before had I been filled with such an awareness of the sacredness of life. I'd just crossed a bridge to the holy of holies."

I was on a roll and couldn't stop. The story itself had taken over and I kept talking almost as if Tom wasn't even there, as if I was crying to the whole universe to see what I'd seen and to recognize how completely this moment altered everything about my life.

"I don't have words to really describe it, but the center of my perceiving dropped through layers of awareness as though I'd fallen into a secret well. As we waited, the yolk-yellow pigment of its eye began to fade. Its life drained into me. I was sad and excited all at the same time. That yellow eye and piercing yellow beak opened a hole in me right in the middle of my chest just where I'd felt the tap when Robert Bly read his poem about the heron, 'We are thirsty for the heron and the lake, the touch of the bill on the water.'

"Eventually I moved out of my stupor and I slowly extended my hand across the canyon between us. I wanted to touch it even though I was still terrified that it would erupt, impale my hand, or put out my eye with its beak. As if a gasping dying bird could understand my deep human emotion, I wanted to show my reverence and acknowledge how in awe I was at this moment. I expected the soft blue color of its feathers to feel like fur or as sensuous as the heron when gliding across the dawn calmed water, but the feathers were cold and stiff.

"It wasn't exactly like the movies where all information is downloaded in an instant, but the connection between the heron and me was the most memorable moment of my life! While in that state I felt that my chest no longer had skin and bones, but was more like an open window covered by a flimsy drape. My chest burned cool and hot at the same time, like a chilly breeze blowing through a blast furnace. I was instantly aware that there were layers like rainbows on top of rainbows of existence I'd never known about. You know, like driving along the mountains between Banff and Jasper and seeing millions of years of strata. I was changed immediately to know that so much more was going on in many levels of existence I'd never experienced before."

I realized that this opening couldn't be described adequately, but the current of the river bore Tom and me along and my words continued to pour out.

"My euphoria slowly turned sad and fearful as I realized that the heron may be in its death throes, and I imagined it must be terrified because this huge human hand was stroking its perilously long neck when it was powerless to move. I wondered if the sounds gurgling from its throat were its death rattle, gasps of fear, or if the heron sensed my complete reverence and was satisfied knowing it had done its work to call me here."

"Shit man, that's amazing! It died while you were stroking its neck? Jesus!" He shuddered in disbelief.

"Not exactly. When I realized that it was still alive and breathing I assumed that being so close to an alien life form might scare it to its death, so as quietly as possible I withdrew and belly-crawled back to the edge of the marsh where I'd left the canoe. I went to the 4th of July party later that evening. I couldn't take my mind off what I'd just experienced. I'd just left a heron dying in the grass!"

••

The Confession

The meeting of two personalities is like the contact of two chemical substances: If there is any reaction, both are transformed.

—C.G. Jung

"What did you do?"

"I went to a 4th of July party at a neighbor's cabin, but I had a hard time dancing with all that was buzzing in my chest. That night I had a profound dream. A wise old taxidermist came to me and told me what I must do to preserve my heron. It was 4:00 in the morning, with a faint light beginning to show in the predawn sky. I jumped out of bed, threw on my contact lenses, grabbed a couple of white plastic trash bags, tossed them into the canoe, and set across the lake to do what the dream instructed.

I beached the canoe at the precise point of the night before and stealthily worked my way to the place of yesterday's encounter, not really expecting to see the heron again. But there it was in the shadows of predawn light, lifelessly sprawled right where I'd left it."

When I got to this part of the story, my voice choked and my eyes welled up again. *It's been twenty-two years and I still choke up when I think about it. Will I ever recover and get normal?* Tom's eyes widened even further and he blinked back his own tears. A spirit of genuine awe filled the space between us. "And Tom, as soon as I saw it lying there, with its head cocked at a weird angle, I looked into the once brilliant yellow eyes and saw dull grey cataracts of death. I burst into tears, sobbing from some place in my being I'd never contacted."

We paused. Tom let himself absorb the scene. In time he asked softly, "What did you do? Did you stuff it and mount it?"

"I tried to stuff it into one of the white garbage bags I took with me, but it was all stiff and spread out and the bag ripped when I tried to put it in. I got it back to the cabin before the family woke up, rearranged our food in the refrigerator, and managed to cram in this five-foot-tall bird with only a few of its charcoal feathers sticking out. Immediately after I got back to town, I called a taxidermist to ask if he would mount it, and he said, 'I can't mount it because it's an endangered bird and it's illegal for me to stuff it! No one else can mount it either!'

"What am I supposed to do with it?"

"'Toss it in the garbage!' and he hung up. I wish I knew then what I know now because I would have handled it much differently. At that point I didn't have the kind of authority to do what I should have done."

"What would you have done differently?"

His question startled me. In the many times I'd told my story no one had asked that question before. I realized immediately that I'd thought there was a right and wrong way to respond to this appearance of a god. The gift of his question let me know that the only thing to do when surprised by the sacred order of the world is to be stunned, incoherent, naive, stupid, and unknowing. There is no way to plan for the appearance of this kind of spiritual reality. There are no coaches to teach us how to respond to Mystery. Nothing can prepare us for such an encounter.

The mesmerizing quality of the heron had swept over Tom and me in the same way a heron, gliding inches above a lake, calms the morning. We'd just entered a sanctuary. All separation between the two of us disappeared, and at least for a while we walked with the same map in the same territory.

I quickly recovered from the momentary nostalgic dip into my old tears. I snuffled, and with the white, freshly laundered linen napkin wiped my way back to the reality of eating breakfast in an open restaurant on the coast of Mexico.

I wanted to go on and on and tell him about the next ten years of my mystical awakening. I wanted to let him know how the herons were a bridge that consistently appeared as a guide both in my dreams and in my waking life, coming to me to verify and assist in the changes that were coming as I adjusted to a new world view. I wanted to tell him of the little blue stone given to me by an Aboriginal Clever Man (Aboriginal way of talking about magicians, medicine men, or shamans) that led me to Australia to work with the Aboriginals in the bush. I wanted to tell him that sometimes we encounter events in our lives that destroy the old way we understand the world and force us to find a new map to guide us into unfamiliar territory. I had much more to talk about. Perhaps in the Canyon, overlooking its majesty, I could continue my story.

Mentally we both sent our attention far out over the ocean while the heron story slipped into the interior place where such treasures rest. When our eyes met again we had shifted gears, and in that safety Tom could now talk about the burden he couldn't bring himself to disclose the night before. On the waking *malecón* in a busy sidewalk cafe it was Tom's turn. Sobered, with hands cupped around his freshened coffee, as a seer might gaze into water to find the hidden wisdom there, he began:

"David, the other day, when we were talking about the bad things we do and the voice of –what did you call it, the shame monster?"

"The shame beast," I nodded.

He paused, circling around the lip of his confession as a marble spirals closer to the center of a concave dish. Truth was coming.

"I told you that after Dad kicked me out of the house, I was heavy into drugs and alcohol. It was the 70's and acid was my drug of choice. I had a younger sister, who like me was trying to get away from Dad's brutality. So....." He exhaled in a huge whoosh, his head dropped a few inches, his eyelids nearly closed, and he moved from anything outside to everything that swirled inside. His shoulders sagged so that nothing supported him other than the structure of his bones, and his face filled with a sad nostalgia. "I had access to all sorts of drugs and introduced her to acid. She'd already been doing a lot of alcohol and pot, but she got hooked on acid. One day she got some bad stuff and had a real nasty trip. Her friend called me in a panic to see if I could help but by the time I got there it was too late. She nearly died, ended up in the hospital with severe brain damage and acute psychosis."

He paused. His unfocused eyes nearly disappeared behind the glossy pools that spilled over the rims of his lower lids. He raised his head to look out over the gently surging surf of the bay, unable to stem the ancient, unshed tears. "She never recovered. She became schizophrenic and has been delusional ever since. She's been in and out of treatment, mental institutions, and prison. I totally blame myself, man. If it hadn't been for me she'd never done the bad drugs."

I watched as his head weaved back and forth, silently debating inside his own mind, trying to shake off the facts of his adult life, wanting to go on, hoping for relief. He swallowed hard several times, trying to hold back what was freight-training to the surface.

After some time passed, he choked out the words, "She lives on the streets now. Addicted to heroin, cocaine, and God only knows what else, sometimes tricking for another fix. Often I'll find her in a halfway house or shelter. She's really whacked. Each month I find her, pay her bills, and cringe when she starts in her schizophrenic babble. It's all my fault."

He sucked in deeply through his nose, aimed his face toward the ceiling, and closed his eyes, "Jesus Christ!" Another long pause, "My father has never forgiven me for fucking her up." His head dropped and he again closed his eyes.

All I could muster was a guttural moan as my head swayed side-to-side imagining the 40 years of his internal torture.

I held this silence, daring not to say anything at that moment. The therapist part of me wanted to say that the secret to dissolving shame was to stand up to the inner voice that blamed him and say, "Yes, I did it and I will do everything in my power to make it better, but I will no longer condemn myself for the mistakes of my youth."

I understood him at that point and began to imagine any way I could help him with his central shame issue without taking on a role as therapist. I also knew that for the rest of our trip I would seek opportunities to strengthen the bridge of trust we'd just built.

This time Tom didn't offer the usual "Fuck it, man" that had become the mantra for this trip. We sat in the dirty, unfinished business of his life, in the near universal human problem of trying to reach the place in his psyche where forgiveness and release could take place. It seemed like forever for his head to slowly scale the cliff of his torment to face the horizon. He took some deep breaths, his face, soft and fluid, turned to me and we just looked at each other. Volumes were spoken in the silent, almost imperceptible nod of our heads as we both blinked back our tears. Just like I'd done when I crossed the chasm between animal and human when the heron died, I gently put my hand across the ravines of our differences, touched his arm, and gave it a tender squeeze.

As we sat there in that profound connection, I understood that in the liberalism of the drug-crazed 70's he'd made some mistakes that had destroyed his sister and traumatized his whole family. "Everyone needs to take responsibility for their own behavior and stop looking for the government to take care of them," he'd shouted in a rage a few nights before during our political slugfest. The harshness of his own guilt made him turn against the world and judge the world as violently as he treated himself. His rabid fundamentalist conservatism was the way he handled his shame as if he needed this brutal condemning fist in his face to keep him reminded of how bad he was. He demanded of the world that it, too, be a fierce judge, forcing everyone to take full responsibility for everything that happened in his or her life. There can be no excuses, no softening of the fact that we're the masters of our fate. He held the whole world to an absolute and unforgiving standard wherein everyone had to make it through on his or her own efforts.

That is why he hated liberalism in any form. He dare not embrace any sort of liberal political stance that would soften individual responsibility. His father's refusal to forgive him shaped his way in the world. I now understood how his unrelenting condemnation of himself formed his politics, and with that, all my animosity dropped away. I no longer feared his diatribes.

The earth shifted between us. My understanding his personal history dissolved the distance between us and provided us solidarity for the days that followed. Our discussion was over for now. Maybe sitting by a campfire overlooking the Canyon, we could pick up some of these deeper threads. In unison we nodded, "Let's hit the road."

Like last night's thunderstorm that freshened the air, our discussion enabled us to head back to the room cleansed by a new-found loyalty to some of the deeper things in each other's lives. By the time we got back to room #208, Jake had crawled out of bed and eaten his Pop Tart breakfast. We checked out of the hotel, dried off our rained-on bikes, packed up, and prepared for the humid day's ride ahead.

••

The Trouble with Maps

Individual people do not have access to absolute knowledge of reality, but only to a set of beliefs they've built up over time about reality. A map can never guarantee that one will find the way out.

—Jan Bucquoy

The trip from Mazatlán to Los Mochis was boring. We had wanted to get on the free road because it took us through the villages and on more interesting curves, but we missed a turn and got diverted to the four-lane toll road that had little to engage our attention. So we compromised and rode the concrete slab, burning up miles as quickly as we could. My attention continuously returned to my intermittent headlight failure but I couldn't find a pattern.

After we ate an early dinner in the hotel in Los Mochis, I spent considerable time in the relative safety of the hidden parking lot stripping everything off my Suzuki to see if I could figure out the headlight's problem. We were headed to Copper Canyon tomorrow and this would be the last chance to fix it. I also knew that a few days later I'd be traveling south alone in Mexico, returning to Ajijic while Tom and Jake headed north to a rally in Idaho. "What's eating you, Dave?" Jake asked when he saw that my seat, gas tank, and fairings were torn off in the parking lot.

"Electrical shorts freak me out," I tried to explain. This was the second time in two days that I'd stripped my bike to bare bones trying to find the problem. "I'm afraid that it will only get worse as I travel. The last thing I want when I'm alone is to have a short that'll start a fire and leave me stranded. Something is wrong and I can't figure out what. The randomness makes me think that it's in the ECU (the computer that manages all the electrical issues of a fuel-injected bike). Why won't the lights work? Besides, down here with all the traffic, it's very important to be as conspicuous as possible. I've still got my visibility driving lights but the last thing I want is a meltdown."

"Here's a solution if that happens," Jake offered. "Because the *Federales* won't tolerate camping on the freeways, just pitch your tent in the median strip. The *Federales* will come by in short order and you can explain to them what you need and they will get you help. It reduces your chances of being robbed."

I tucked that bit of information away but was quite disappointed that he didn't dive into the problem with me. A bolt had worked loose and fallen off his windshield and I pulled away from my project to help him fix his, hoping he'd reciprocate. I'd assumed that because he was a mechanical engineer of some renown he ought to know about a motorcycle's electrical system. Unfortunately, not only was that assumption grossly inaccurate, it would complicate things later on.

After I'd torn the headlight switch apart, checked all the wiring harnesses I could get to, pulled all the fuses, and put in new ones, I had no more ideas how to find the problem. I grew more concerned that some terminal cancer was eating at the belly of my Suzi. My tools couldn't reach the depth of what had infected it.

"We gotta figure out where we're going tomorrow. Come on, let's get to work," Tom announced when we retired to our small two-bed "suite" that had barely enough space for the extra rollaway.

I had a basic road map of Mexico and Jake had a larger map with a few more details than mine. He also had an 8.5 x 11 photocopy of a hand-drawn map we'd looked at when we were back in Ajijic. It had been crumpled and copied so many times, that the names of the towns were hard to read. Jake reminded us, "I found a guy who knows a guy who has been there and drew this map. He said it's pretty good. Here, we can just follow this." He tossed it on the bed.

Two problems emerged immediately! First, none of us had any idea about the territory we were about to enter. In all our preparation, none of us had researched the area to know what the terrain was like, what to expect in terms of weather, what kind of roads we'd be on, how far from one campground to the next, and where we could buy food, water, or fuel. The large, general map of Mexico contained no details of terrain or size of towns. The hand-drawn map was not to scale and was scattered with some nearly indecipherable scribbles Perhaps, they might help: "much gravel; be careful of large trucks they will push you off the road; dangerous crossing after rain," etc. These notes written at the bottom of the page relieved our anxiety a bit because it affirmed that someone had been there

The second problem became apparent when Tom and I spread our meager information on the bed. Jake disappeared into the music on his iPod.

"Get your ass over here and help us figure out where we ought to go!" Tom demanded.

Jake pulled the earphone out of his ear. "What?"

"Get your ass over here and help us out!"

"Naw, fuck it. You guys go ahead and figure it out. It doesn't matter to me where we go. You guys decide."

Because Jake was the one who had the passion for the trip and organized it, and the one who found a friend who had a friend who had a map, I figured he had an idea of where we were going and how to get there. Most ironically, while back in Ajijic, I'd been uncharacteristically passive and rather than researching and understanding all the details, I had stepped to the background and decided to trust their planning. After all, the two of them had been planning the trip for almost a year. I was new to Mexico and was content to be the tag-along for the adventure.

Whereas both Tom and I rode on Jake's shirttail to get to the Canyon, it became apparent that he had little use for the details that would make for a good ride. Like the two of them I assumed, based solely on our male competence, we would be able to handle anything that came our way. I looked forward to the mystery of our trip because part of the joy of being on an adventure comes from the courage to ride into the unknown and figure out what to do with what shows up.

The legend for the roads we'd be traveling showed thin yellow lines, indicating paved but not necessarily good highways. It seemed a simple task to plot a rough course from El Fuerte to Creel, the main town on the north lip of the Canyon. Our assumption regarding the quality of the roads came from our previous experiences of riding in the United States or Canada, where in the national forests there were always provisions for adventurers like us. Squinting in the dim hotel room light, I pointed to the map, "It looks like we can turn off here at El Fuerte, head east, and here, head north on this road."

"Yeah, but what if it's not a good road? Maybe it'll be gravel and I've told you before I don't do dirt! I've already broken my neck and I have a hip replacement. If I drop a bike up there, it will be very bad. The doc told me that a motorcycle accident would be awful for me. A wreck could pull the bone away from my metal hip."

There were only occasional points of correspondence between our road atlas and the homemade map. I looked at Tom, "If this was drawn by a Canadian, these might be kilometers, not miles. Do you have any idea which?"

I looked again at the official Mexico roadmap, "It's a yellow road on the map except for a section of grey that indicates a not-so-good road. Up there, nearer to Croix, the scribbled note on the friend's map says: 'OK road. Dusty with log trucks that will push you off the road. Use extreme caution. Many steep cliffs.' That sounds too difficult; maybe this one down here is better. What do you think, Jake?"

"What?" pulling an earphone away from his left ear, "I told you, figure it out. I don't care."

Obviously, because his skill level was so much higher than ours he had no worry about being able to negotiate anything he came across. Not so for Tom or me. We were not experienced off-road riders and wanted to avoid dirt roads. Maybe I could tolerate a few miles of gravel, but even the thought of off-roading sent shivers up my spine. The closest thing I'd come to riding in the dirt was on my little trail bike when I was 15 and watching motocross races on TV.

After a couple of hours looking at the maps, in vain hoping to touch a layer of magical knowledge that would indicate what would be the best road, we put away our maps. "El Fuerte is a modest town and the railroad starts there to go into the Barrancas. There ought to be a map there. Let's stop there tomorrow and pick one up." I conceded.

"Good idea." In the morning we would find a map that would reveal a true picture of the territory. I didn't sleep well that night. My dreams didn't help.

As in all Mexican towns, the church and adjacent stores frame the central plaza of El Fuerte. *¿Dónde podemos comprar una mapa de las Barrancas del Cobre?* became our mantra as we talked to as many locals as we could. Even the "Chamber of Commerce" offered no help. No maps. Even though El Fuerte was referred to as the jumping off place for the Canyon, we couldn't locate a Forest Service map with legible print indicating elevations, intersections, camping spots, panoramic vistas, etc. None of the locals had any idea what we were talking about! They were sitting next to one of the world's most stunning geographical features and all we got in return for our fervent requests were blank stares.

The only indication of what to expect was given by the manager at a local hotel who said, "The rains have started. You're on motorcycles and may be OK for now, but soon all the roads will be impassable." But still no map.

In the old movie *Butch Cassidy and the Sundance Kid* the two heroes are caught between a precipice that falls to a river below and the Marshal and his men who finally have them trapped. They look at each other, look at the peril of jumping off the cliff into the water, and look back at the relentless Marshal with guns drawn. In unison they yell as they jump to their certain death. It was like that with us as well. Trapped between uncertainty and our desire to get there before the rains came, we left the main road in El Fuerte with no better information than we had months ago. "Fuck it. Let's go for it."

••

Abandon Hope, All Ye Who Enter Here

*What is required of us is that we live the difficult and learn to deal with it.
In the difficult are the friendly forces, the hands that work on us.*

—Joseph Campbell

We headed east, not north. When Dante passed through the entrance to hell he read the warning over the gate, "Abandon hope, all ye who enter here." It would not be long before those words became the reality I lived for days. We were on a quest for Beauty. The closer we got to the Canyon, the more our excitement to get there took over. Within four miles outside of El Fuerte the asphalt thinned out and the road worsened into a dusty, potholed obstacle course. Gravel became boulders, dips in the road became small ditches, slight rises in elevation became steep inclines, little erosions became serious ruts, and in time random wet spots became standing water or long mud puddles. Because I'd seen a yellow coded road on Mexico's official map, I figured we'd soon return to blacktop. Our destination, our treasure, our commitment to get there, superseded all the warnings that suggested we turn back. Better roads would surely have to turn up again, just look at the map. I ground my teeth in determination, tried to find a way to see through my dust-covered visor, and rode on. I screwed down my eyes to narrow slits, blinking rapidly to flush the grit from underneath my contact lenses. It would be hours before I was sure we'd taken the wrong road, but by then we were too far in to easily retreat. The highway had deteriorated from asphalt to terror.

Our seminal problem was that we had decided to ride this direction and put our faith in the hand-drawn scribbled map. We held onto this choice as if our lives depended on its accuracy. To have an idea of where we were going was far easier on us than having no idea at all.

Off in the horizon we could make out some mountains

through the haze. Maybe the Canyon was just beyond that. I had visions that we were finally headed for the panoramas. The trouble with this idea was that the hoped-for vistas became the focal point and we failed to consider the deteriorating condition of the road. Had we said, let's explore this road to see if it will take us to where we want to go, we would have left open the possibility to turn around if it became more and more perilous. As soon as our minds were made up, our options closed down, data and details no longer entered the equation, and any extraneous information was filtered out. Tragically the combination of our assumptions and the hand-drawn map, not the terrain, told us where we were and where we ought to be.

I was riding ahead of the guys at this point, but Jake grew impatient with my awkward attempts to get my 550-pound gear-loaded motorcycle to negotiate the slippery sand and gravel washboard road. I wanted to go straight, but the bike wanted to follow the soft sand into the ruts that were sure to throw me off. My front wheel wandered, disconnected from the rest of the bike like a headstrong horse fighting the rider to go where it wanted. I might as well have been riding on grease. Jake stood on his foot pegs and with a wild whoop like a cowboy on a bucking bronco, screamed from underneath his helmet "Yee haw!" as he blasted past me, 30 mph faster than I was riding. The grin on his dusty face said it all. It seemed effortless for him and as soon as the huge rooster tail of dust settled, I wrapped my fists tightly against my handgrips and, terrified, tried unsuccessfully to match his torrid pace.

Riding a motorcycle on gravel roads is like driving on ball bearings. In Mexico, the bane of off-road riders is the six-inch deep red dust the consistency of talcum powder that hides any rocks or ruts underneath. It is deceptively slick. Not only does the dust kick up so you can't see anything, it throws the bike willy-nilly in whatever direction it wants. Riding out of control in those crappy sections became my worst fear! Surely this was just a temporary section of rough road and we would soon return to the comfort of asphalt. It slowly dawned on me that the horrible road we were on was the road we were on.

"How in the hell do you ride in this stuff?" I asked Jake after watching him fearlessly fly across the rudimentary road. "My front end feels like it wants to slide off the road. I feel like I'm driving on ice."

"Stand on the foot pegs, lean back and keep your weight off the front tire."

"That makes no sense to stand up. If you do that your center of gravity is higher and that will make it harder to control."

"In a way, it lowers your center of gravity because when you stand on the pegs, the weight is transferred lower on the bike. Besides, your legs become shock absorbers and that keeps the tires on the dirt better. If you're sitting on the bike, the suspension bounces you off your butt and when you come back to the seat the shocks now have to absorb your sorry ass rather than work to keep the tires on the road."

I continued to test that idea as the day wore on. I'd seen off-road videos, and indeed, on this kind of road they all stood up. It didn't feel right or comfortable but I was in no position to say it didn't work. Up on his foot pegs Jake roared off again, "Watch and learn!"

After an hour or more, we became even more disoriented, and couldn't make sense of our map, so in our mangled half-Spanish we asked a group of six men at a crossroads if they could help. We thought they told us to go back five miles to take a different road at the fork. We backtracked only to discover that we had misunderstood their instructions and had to return again to the same fork where we had received the original misinformation.

It became apparent to us that when we'd asked for directions the Mexicans, having no clue what we were asking, would give us initial blank stares and then a quick flurry of words. This was simply their land. For them there was no objectified place called *"Barrancas del Cobre."* The soiled white paper map with handwritten names didn't correspond to anything the villagers had ever seen. With their kind of nature-grown instinct they didn't need maps! Most Westerners have a place in mind when they think of a feature of nature, but that notion of leaving here to get there is absent from rural Mexicans. Life is local, tied to here, and one does not dream of getting to another place called "there."

Rather than ask for directions to the Canyon, we had better luck when we picked a specific town and asked for instructions to get there. On the map, one of the biggest dots was a town called Morelos and it became our destination when we asked if we were on the right road.

Frustrated with this loss of two hours and twenty miles, I took the lead to recover the ground we'd covered. For a while I tried the new stand-up technique, riding adventure-style, trying to learn how to balance the bike while standing up on the pegs rather than sitting on the seat.

Riding in front I didn't have to eat that gritty red dust. I came to a steep, deeply rutted downhill section that had a hard right-hand corner at the bottom. Loose sand covered the washed-out corner, and I knew I had to keep out of the tire-swallowing rut. My bike didn't have knobby tires that were designed to bite through the soft dirt for traction. They were designed for riding on pavement. The advertisement said they were designed for 80% street use and 20% dirt. They lied. They were absolutely worthless in gravel, dust, and ruts, and as I was soon to learn, dangerous in mud! After I scrubbed enough speed off to get down the hill, I carefully applied the gas to get the weight off the front end, but the squirrelly street tires slid on the sand, fell into the rut and sent my bike and me hard to the ground.

With no time to break my fall, I banged my head full force on the rocks. I was on the ground, my right ankle pinned under my saddlebag, my head aimed down the ravine. On the way down, my foot got caught on the saddlebag and violently twisted my body. I think I would have broken an ankle or torn a knee except that I was able to twist my upper body backward so I didn't tear my leg off.

It hurt. By the time Jake and Tom came down the hill and got their bikes on their kickstands, I'd managed to get out from underneath to look at my poor bike. I'd smashed my $300 driving lights, the right-side blinker, and buggered the mirror. My crash bars prevented damage to the tank, but I went down hard enough to bend them in towards the frame. My brake pedal was twisted, but most of all, my up to now virgin bike had been damaged, my right ankle and knee mangled and throbbing. My first trip off asphalt and I failed to keep the rubber side down. We had been on this road for less than two hours. This was only my second unplanned get-off in forty-seven years of riding motorcycles. I was embarrassed.

After I dropped my bike in the corner I figured I'd really have to work to keep my eyes up and forward because the mind acutely remembers accidents. I headed up the hill still trying to clear the fog out of my head. Even though I knew the principal motorcycle safety rule, "Look where you want to go," every corner produced a replay of my previous crash and sent icy spikes of fear shooting through me. Try as I might I couldn't keep my eyes ahead and not look down at the rock or washout. My focus was drawn to the danger rather than to the challenge of the slope ahead.

When I was teaching motorcycle safety we drove the mantra, "Keep your eyes up! Look through the corner!" into the heads of our students. However, now that I was afraid of hurting myself again, I had a compulsion to look straight down at the scary rocks on the ground. That invariably upset my balance because keeping my eyes looking ups toward the horizon is essential to maintain equilibrium. My fear drew my focus to the rocks below, which upset my stability, which caused more fear.

Could I make the transition? Could I use my fright to remind me that my terror came from memory, not from what was going on in the moment? This is exactly what I have been teaching my psychotherapy clients for years! Fear comes from a story of what could happen or comes from a memory of what did happen. Those stories are useless when the task is to climb the next hill, cross the next stream. *Look where you want to go! Stand up on the foot pegs! Get the weight on the back wheel! Pour on the power!*

Riding and successful therapy parallel each other at this point. When clients become aware and break the automatic and unconscious reliving of the past drama and bring their attention to the here and the now, they're free to make choices. The unconscious scenarios that dominate the inner movie of the mind determine what we see and how we feel. All of us live much of our life guided by these memory-driven stories and it seems natural to look to the past as if what happened can necessarily predict and control the future. But when riding, that which seems natural is disastrous because focus on the error takes attention away from what the now requires.

Later on Tom was riding between Jake and me. Up ahead, the recent rains had flooded the banks of the stream and the water was flowing down the road. Without hesitation Jake, always happy with a challenge, stood on his pegs, gassed his bike and flew right through the 100-footlong section, sending steam and spray far to the side. He war-whooped when he got to the other side of the water and stopped to see how Tom and I would handle this chunk of horror. This first water crossing was gut check time for Tom. As soon as he hit the stream, he careened off a submerged rock, swerved hard to the left, and went sprawling headfirst into foot-deep water. He got up sputtering, absolutely drenched. We both rushed to his aid and stood up his steaming bike.

I didn't want to have the same thing happen to me, so I paddle-walked my bike through the basketball-sized boulders at the edge of the road and still managed to drop my bike once more before I made it to the other side. Tom's violent headfirst into the water and the real possibility of the motorcycle sucking in water and ruining the engine freaked both Tom and me. The rest of the day we struggled through water hazards, steep and washed-out roads, boulders, and choking dust. Our anxiety was made worse because we'd both had fairly serious wrecks.

Jake's superiority as an off-road rider became more apparent because by the end of the first day, Tom had dropped his bike twice more and I hit the ground three more times, while Jake kept his BMW upright. Exhausted, we finally found a place to pitch our tents on uneven ground. We couldn't find good tinder and struggled a long time to start a fire to dry Tom's still soggy riding gear. I feasted on some smashed granola bars I rescued from my tank bag, Jake chomped on his nutritional mainstay, Pop Tarts, and Tom, preoccupied with drying out, decided not to eat anything. We were in fact too tired to eat. Setting up camp, we didn't speak much and, with only the stony ground to sit on, we didn't find much comfort in the fire or opportunity for fellowship.

The mistake we'd made to ride this direction became more obvious to me when I carefully compared the map to the terrain we had already crossed. I'd put my GPS away as soon as we left El Fuerte because it no longer offered any information about the roads we were on. I turned it on after we set up camp to see if by chance it could give me any clues what was ahead. It didn't show the roads, only endless ridges and mountains. I looked at the clouds descending over the ridges ahead, the evidence of heavy rain where we were camped, and the GPS view of much steeper climbs and mountain range after mountain range ahead of us. All the information I gathered pointed to several more days of the same agony we had just inched through. We had come a mere 30 or 40 miles into a journey on a road that was at least ninety miles longer, and the map we'd been using was useless!

The days are longest in late June, so it took a long time for the descending darkness to match the sullen gloom that settled over us. As the air cooled and the humidity enveloped us in a growing fog, the increasing emotional tension among the three of us became more complex. We went to bed hungry, but finding food was not the first issue I wanted to confront.

Because there wasn't enough level ground to pitch three tents, Tom and I shared one. I waited for sleep to claim me. It didn't come. We both tossed and turned at the edge of sleep for hours. Just when I might have been able to make the transition into sleep, he would rustle in his bag and I'd wake up again. Unable to quiet our weary minds from reliving the dramas of the day, sore all over from having been thrown off our bikes, leg muscles aching from standing on our foot pegs all day, and fighting the tendency to slide down to the bottom of our tent which was pitched on a slope, we stopped battling for sleep. Heavy dew soaked the tent. At four in the morning I whispered, "You awake?"

"Yeah. I can't sleep! I don't think I've slept at all. I'm really sore."

"Same for me. I've been lying here thinking that we should turn around and go back. I looked at the GPS last night and saw nothing but canyon after canyon ahead of us."

"Your GPS shows us the road?"

"No, it doesn't give any details, it just gives the satellite view. We are at 2900 feet elevation here and we need to climb to 8,000 feet. I see clouds hovering on the tops of the ridges ahead and I imagine more rain. Even if it's just the light rain we have now, the roads are gonna get slicker as we go on. We're going to go up and down for God knows how long."

He sensed where I was headed, "I'm not going to turn around. No way am I going back through that shit we came through today." He shuddered at the memory of dumping his bike in the water. "Whatever is ahead can't be any worse than we came through today! I'm not going back through that water!"

"No! No! Use your head. We already know what we came

through and can surely get across it again. We'll just take it slower and help each other out. Come on." My appeal didn't cut through his fear.

"I'm not going to do it. Nothing can be as bad as that crap! If you and I leave without Jake, we'll never make it."

Tom had decided to forge ahead. I'd hoped that if he and I could agree, we could persuade Jake to turn back with us. I couldn't believe it because earlier on he was so firm when he talked about his hip replacement and broken neck and would not put himself in peril again, but now, part way in, he would have nothing to do with turning around and getting out. Fear does strange things to the mind. God, I hated his stubbornness, especially because it was an irrational reaction to his fear.

In the morning, thinking I'd have better luck with Jake, I walked up the hill and as he was packing his tent I tried, "I talked to Tom last night and tried to persuade him that it would be better for us if we turn back."

He bristled. "Yeah, I heard you guys and wondered what you were talking about."

"I want to state my case." I tried logic. "Tom has had a hip replacement and I don't want to see him endanger himself. Maybe we can find another way in. It's raining up ahead. I see hundreds of valleys and ridges on the GPS, and we have to climb to 8,000 feet." I repeated what I'd said a few hours before.

He set his jaw. "Nope! I ain't turning back."

Their absolute refusal left me with only two options. I could split from them and return alone, which I deemed extremely unsafe, or stay with the group, which seemed disastrous but at least there would be strength in numbers. If I dropped my bike while riding alone, it would be impossible for me to right it by myself. So I overpowered the strong instinct to return and decided to stay with the safety of riding together. Though on the outside I decided to continue with them, everything inside kept warning me to find another way.

While we were getting ready to mount up, Tom confronted

Jake, "You have to bring up the rear!"

"Na, you guys are too slow. If I follow you, I'll crash!"

"Yeah, but when we crash, we won't be able to get our bikes up. If you're behind, you can help us! Otherwise, we will be SOL."

In the middle of the night we'd discussed the advantages of Jake leading or following, debating between following him through dicey sections in order to follow his tracks and find the best way through, or having him ride behind us to help us if we had trouble. We decided we would be in more trouble if we crashed behind him or ended up at the bottom of the cliff. Tom's insistence to have him follow us reflected the extreme fear he and I shared.

We both knew that in these conditions the two of us were not physically strong enough to pick our bikes up because we always crashed on steep sections or where there was no traction. After we'd both dropped our bikes a number of times we realized it would always take three of us to pick them up again. Jake was as strong as the two of us put together, but it was clear that we were becoming a drag on him and could feel his growing annoyance at carrying the weight of two lesser riders. Reluctantly Jake finally agreed, "Yeah, I guess you're right."

We had awakened sluggish but by relinquishing my hope to return and having talked Jake into taking our needs into account, we'd managed to cross a threshold before we left that morning. We realized that like a braided rope, we needed each other. From then on, even though I was aware of the constant pressure of his BMW churning behind me, I was pleased that he had overcome his selfishness and had taken our concerns into account.

Once I'd decided to continue, I knew that I needed more than ever to stay focused on the driving challenges that showed up. Not long after we'd broken camp and headed out, Tom was leading and I was following. The roads were damp from the night's gentle rain. Initially only a few puddles dotted the road, but as time went on, the roads got steeper and wetter. I drove around one corner and the road texture turned to super slick red mud. Try as I might to keep forward momentum, the rear tire broke loose, spun me towards the downhill side of the road and immediately I went down. I was going only 10-15 mph, but the bike went down so quickly that I banged my head hard again.

Jake and I got on the side of the bike to stand it up, but the road was as slick as ice so when we tried to get it up, it simply slid on its side until the tires hit the edge of the upside of the hill. We managed to get it up but now it was standing in the five-inch-deep muddy soup at the edge of the road. It fell over again as I tried to get my leg across the seat. I spun my way out of the ditch, but in so doing ended up sliding across the road sidewise and went down again. I'd had it! Any resolve to stay with this horrible trip evaporated. We stood it up again and I found a tree stump to sit on to collect myself. By that time, Tom on his mud-coated BMW had returned.

"Guys, I don't want to go on. It's just as I said. We are going to have more and more difficulty moving ahead. It has been raining a lot here and the roads won't get any better!"

Tom shut off his bike, "Listen, Dave, I've been up ahead, and just around the corner the roads get better again. It's just a short distance where the road is like this. I promise."

I knew it was BS. No one knew what was ahead, but both he and Jake urged me to go on for just a bit. I didn't have a better plan. I'd already decided that I couldn't change their minds and that I'd have to suck it up and continue to ride. I wanted a rational discussion and didn't want to become a whining drag that created more conflict. The journey, like a python, had us gripped by its backward facing teeth and was swallowing us whole. Every attempt we made to pull back drove its fangs in deeper. It couldn't release us even if it wanted to. And it didn't want to.

Jake must have figured that my resolve to continue was waning and, thinking it was time to educate us on the nuances of riding in mud, told us, "Truck tires ride in the center of the left and right tracks and kick the loose rocks and gooey stuff to either side of the puddle. You'll find best traction in the middle where the water will be the deepest. Drive in the deepest part of the rut. The bottom will be firm there. Give it some gas and get your weight off the front tire."

We didn't have the luxury of time to move from one under-standing of the world to another. What had to be done had to be done now. Where to find traction and firm footing, though second nature to Jake, was a new idea for Tom and me but, sure to his teaching, when I applied it over the next few miles it proved him to be accurate. Trusting the direction and momen-tum of the bike and not relying on steering, getting the weight off the front tire, pouring on the power and heading deepest into the unknown was helpful and in the ensuing miles, I be-gan to enjoy some confidence in this new attack mode. I had to score one for trusting the thrust, relying on momentum, and not fussing so much with the handlebars. This road was where I had to be and I had to give myself over to what it demanded. So what if we had made decisions that led us to chasms of di-saster, I needed to get on.

··

Life at the Ledge

Mankind owns four things
that are no good at sea.
Rudder, Anchor, Oar
and the fear of going down.

—Antonio Machado

Both Jake and his bike were equipped for this type of ride. Because of his oversized tank he had no worries about fuel, but Tom and I were concerned because we'd driven a whole day without finding a place to buy gas. On the highway my bike had a range of 250 miles before needing fuel and Tom had already proven that his bike wouldn't go nearly as far as mine before needing to fill up. However, grinding along in first and second gear, I had no idea how far we could go before running out. "Keep your eyes peeled. I need to find gas."

"Yeah, me too" chimed in Tom. An hour later in a small clearing where two roads intersected, we stopped to buy water and Snickers bars at a traditional *tienda*. These stores were no more than a small room tacked on the side of a structure that sold 100% junk food. Scrawled in black pen on a paper sign nailed to the door we saw *gasolina*. I looked around for a pump. Maybe there was a gravity feed tank in the back I couldn't see.

"Do you have gas, *Señorita?*" Tom asked the storekeeper. "*Sí, señor.*" She looked at me, "*¿Cuántos litros?*"

"Fill it until the pump clicks off." I didn't know. I just wanted a full tank. She looked at me dumbfounded. "Ten liters," I guessed.

I followed her to a shed in the back across cinder-red ground that was still moist from the previous night's rain. The scent from the pine trees and the needle-covered red dirt behind her store reminded me of the forests back in Oregon. It was a relief to be out of the dust for just a bit. She picked up a white plastic bucket from the dirt, slid a piece of plastic off a 55-gallon drum, dipped the bucket, and pulled out what she figured was 10 liters. She handed me a funnel made from a liter coke bottle with the bottom cut off. I held it over my tank opening while she poured what I hoped was gas from the bucket. A fair percentage of the gas made it into my tank while the rest splashed on my leather pants and ran down the sides of the tank. I worried about the quality of the gas.

When I returned, Tom had obviously complained and I overheard Jake say without looking up, "If he is going too slow, screw it, just go around him. You've got to keep up your momentum!" By now, each of us had settled into our own pace for picking through the rock, ruts, and rubble, and even though their frustration weighed on me, I knew that I had to ride at a speed that worked for me. I'd lectured to my motorcycle students how important it is, when riding with a group, to ride within their own limits. "Ride your own ride." The temptation, especially for new riders, is to keep up with the group and end up riding beyond their ability. Here against the vertical cliffs, we knew it was important to stay close enough to be in visual contact in case of a crash, which meant we constantly struggled to adjust our speed to each other.

Tom took the lead from the gas stop. The fumes from my gas-soaked pants were still reaching my nose when we headed up a particularly steep boulder-strewn incline. Always, whenever a section of road steepened, the ruts got deeper, the washouts became more severe, the big rocks that protruded were more pronounced, and the ride became more precarious. The rough obstacle course demanded intricate focus, balance, forward vision, and judicious throttle control.

Threading my way through the rutted boulder field on what seemed like a near vertical face, I saw a particularly ominous section. In the middle of this very precipitous grade, a ledge of granite crossed the road. It looked like the steep slope of a breaking wave, a monster that guarded a secret chamber, flexing its muscles, glaring at me, daring this dinky mosquito on a motorcycle to get past. If I didn't have enough speed to stand the motorcycle up on its rear wheel and lift the front wheel off the ground, the center of the bike would hang up on the lip of the rock and bring me to an immediate and grinding stop. On my right a rock wall left me no exit and to my left was an OH-MY-GOD sheer drop-off.

My rational mind knew that I had to trust the momentum, keep the revs up, give it enough throttle, and "see" all the way over the ledge. Like golfers or baseball players who are taught to "look through the ball," overcoming this obstacle was no different. *Look through to the other side! Stand up, get ready to hit the throttle, lift the front tire over the ledge, and let your speed carry you over the top! Get it right this time!* I told my mind. But my schizophrenic twin insisted, talking back to me faster than I could shut it up, *Hit the brakes! Stop this nonsense! What in the hell are you doing here! Get out! Go home!*

Acting entirely on its own, unable to decide which side to obey, my throttle hand froze! Without enough speed or power to let my momentum carry me over the top, only my front wheel made it over the lip of that monstrous wave. The center of the bike smacked the rock and I slammed to a dead stop. My feet couldn't reach the ground. The bike went over, pitching me towards the edge of the precipice.

"Are you OK?" Jake had stopped his bike, taken off his helmet and had run up to me, sweat dripping off his face.

This time I was more embarrassed than hurt, "Yeah. Damn, I saw that ledge coming and I just froze."

Meanwhile Tom had disappeared ahead, which left the two of us to slide the Suzuki up onto the road away from the cliff. We grunted and groaned, cussed and heaved together and managed to get it far away enough from the ravine so we could get under the bike and stand it up.

Swearing seemed to help. I didn't blame him for his impatience. I'd lost count of the number of times he had to stop to help either Tom or me right our bikes and push on. Jake is a brute of a man, fiercely strong and determined, and without his immense strength we would never have made it as far as we did.

By this time of the day, after righting our bikes so many times and standing on the foot pegs, my legs had turned into wet noodles. My mind was in worse shape. While we were sitting on the road, heaving from the exertion and our bikes clinking as they cooled off, we looked across the ravine of the hill we'd been climbing and saw hundreds of trees ripped away from the steep slope. We followed the trail of the recently slashed ground, and 400 feet beneath we saw the freshly crumpled skeleton of a dump truck that had tumbled down this mountainside, lying there like an insect belly up in its death throes. I couldn't imagine what business a dump truck would have on this nearly impassable section of road. We just shook our heads. We didn't need to say much. The twisted truck, washed-out road, and stripped section of forest said it all.

Worse, I still had to surmount the rock face that now looked taller than the Matterhorn.

I didn't need another lesson but Jake hissed between clenched teeth, "Stand on the pegs, drive the rear tire deep into the dirt until you bruise it. Carry enough momentum so the front tire lifts over the edge of the rock and as soon as the tire clears the lip, throw your body weight forward over the handlebars and the rear wheel will follow!" His exasperation was nearly as strong as my fear as I gathered my resolve to surmount the outcropping. Would this be the place where he called it quits? How much longer before his patience runs out and he leaves me in his dust to fend for myself? I hated the feeling of being weak, and it felt worse to be a burden.

Even though I was exhausted by this time of day, I still had to find both physical and mental strength to get out of this mess. In the few minutes before I mounted up again I remembered a particularly life-strengthening episode that came during a horrific time during my awakening. I'd been acutely paralyzed by my fear of continuing into the unknown, and longed to return to the safe comfort of what used to work for me. A wise old architect appeared in my dream and with thundering authority declared, "DO NOT BE DONE!!! IF YOU TURN BACK NOW IT WILL GO BADLY FOR YOU! Your course is to be alone. Your dreams will continue to instruct you and encourage you when your energies are exhausted." I had to ride my own ride. No one had yet traveled my unique territory. With no manuals, I would be taught through the living of my life what I should or shouldn't do, could or couldn't do.

True to the architect's teaching, my dreams became a constant guide and companion. I learned by going where I had to go.

Right here, facing the Matterhorn, my fear, and yearning to be rescued, the principle of countersteering meant that I must continue to steer against the instinct and desire to return to asphalt. I could feel the echo of my dream in Jake's instructions, "Do not be done. Pour on the power! Don't wish to be somewhere else!" Life and motorcycling are always about finding traction.

I backed the bike down the hill and while I was revving up my motor, gathering up my courage, I recalled Carl Jung's answer to his grandson's query about what makes a good sailor: "You have to learn how to curse the wind!"

With the power of a curse in my arsenal, I swallowed hard, pulled in the clutch, put it in first gear, and squeezed both front and back brakes hard to keep from sliding backwards. The sinister twin in my brain warned me, *Look at the crushed truck lying beneath you on your left. You're going to die.* I turned away from that one and I put all my energy in my voice and with a shout that was heard across the land I bellowed, "YOU BASTARD SON OF A BITCH! CURSED BE THE DAY YOU WERE BORN AND THE HORSE THAT BROUGHT YOU HERE!"

I popped the clutch and scrambled up that steep incline, accelerated, stood on the pegs, attacked the hill, and just when the front tire lifted over the lip I threw my weight forward, the back tire found its grip, bruising the rocks, and in a matter of seconds I was back on the road again, wondering if the driver of the dump truck was able to bail out or if his life was crushed along with the truck.

I thought about this incident many times later when drawing parallels to some of life's more challenging questions. We learn things from heroes that have gone before and use their resolve when ours is too small. But how do you know when you're supposed to stop? How do you determine if it's the fussy voice of fear that unnecessarily paralyzes, or the voice of deeper wisdom that is calling for a legitimate retreat? How do you close that troublesome eye that insists on seeing all the danger when you know your task is to focus on where you want to go?

Awareness was the goal I couldn't reach. The more tired I became, the less control I had. The dreaded "what ifs" boiled through my mind without interruption. *What would Gloria and my kids feel when they found out I was at the bottom of a cliff too mangled to retrieve? What would it be like tumbling on the way to the bottom of the cliff? Would I suffer on the way down?* All sorts of useless scenarios crowded against my dwindling reserves. Out loud I'd repeat, "You go where you look! Look where you want to go!" My mantra didn't work very well.

I couldn't rescue myself from my impaired state because I didn't recognize that my judgment was compromised. It was impossible to *think* my way out of such a state. Water, food, and most important, rest, were the only things that could return me to normal thinking. Uncomfortable and unhappy, I lost contact with my intuition, reverted to an unreliable part of the brain, and fell prey to its story. I was taking directions from a map I didn't choose. When I needed to see most, I was blinded by my own blindness. A functional headlight wouldn't help me now.

Jung loved it when his clients came to these situations in which they couldn't move forward or backward. He said,

"When you are up against a wall, be still and put down roots like a tree, until clarity comes from deeper sources to see over the wall." My stillness was far away.

••

Under the Mud

*It is by going down into the abyss that we recover the treasures of life.
Where you stumble, there lies your treasure.*

—Joseph Campbell

*An old lady told William James that the earth rested on the back of a huge
turtle. "But, my dear lady," Professor James asked, as politely as possible,
"what holds up the turtle?" "Ah," she said, "That's easy. He is standing on
the back of another turtle." "Oh, I see, but would you be so good as to tell
me what holds up the second turtle?" "It's no use, Professor," said the old
lady, realizing he was trying to lead her into a logical trap. "It's turtles-tur-
tles-turtles, all the way down!"*

Tom had paused up ahead to wait for us to catch up. We
began to develop a sense of when one of us had had trouble negotiating a tricky section of road. When either Tom or I
managed to get through a challenging section first, we'd stop
to make sure all was well with the riders behind. After topping
the ledge and feeling more confident, I took the lead again.

I'd successfully replaced the stay-out-of-the-water strategy
with trusting what Jake had taught us. Now rather than hesitate when I came to standing water, imagining what tire-grab-
bing monsters lurked hidden in the elongated water-filled ruts,
I applied his counsel that the best traction was in the unseen.
Just like in countersteering, where the instinct to turn away
from trouble pushes the rider directly into its path, diving into
the center of the dangerous mud puddle proved to be the best
option.

With the weight off the front tire, the bike's momentum directed the steering and the bike didn't get tossed around when
the front tire hit something slick. It was best to attack the deeper part of the trenches, sending spray, mud, and any loose gravel to the side. Against the instinct to ride on the visible parts
of a muddy road, I found the best traction in the middle of the
parallel ruts. Thought and instinct collide not only in riding,

but also in nearly every conflict in life.

This lesson in traction had parallels to how my life changed after the Great Blue Heron died in my arms. Each night, I was graced with profound new dreams, daily I was flooded by synchronistic experiences, poetry, music, and fresh insights. I was gifted with near constant reminders that an informing presence operated alongside my consciousness. My sense of the sacred had never been more acute. The flood of new perceptions split me wide open.

For example, in the beginning phases of my awakening, when in almost constant wonder, I went for nearly nine months without a single new psychotherapy client. My caseload dwindled to the point where I couldn't pay my bills. I would often see only one or two clients during the day, but was satisfied to sit wide-eyed for hours in contact with deep spiritual realms. Though euphoric, I was not making any money. I began to feel desperate but still believed that living so close to "spirit" would guarantee continued financial success. It made no sense to me why, when I was being so opened by such an expansion, the forces behind the spiritual opening would abandon me and leave my family and me destitute.

Frustrated as I'd ever been, caught between financial poverty on one hand and riches of the psyche on the other, I drove home one night absolutely spent and furious with the forces that were taking me through this. It was odd and I wondered if some divine hand had cut off my telephone line and refused me any new clients. On my way home I railed against the Great Mystery, I screamed at the dream, I shook my fist in rage and literally tore my voice to shreds cursing the day this all started, "I don't want any more fucking dreams! I don't want a single new insight! I don't want another poem, another song, or another magical appearance of a heron! I simply want to know what is going on. Don't you dare give me one more image that I have to interpret! I want it clean. I want it simple. I want it clear!"

I managed that evening to hide my rage from my family, but

I carried my Tasmanian devil intensity into my sleep. Then at exactly 2:00 in the morning I was awakened by a voice as clear as if there was a loudspeaker in my bedroom, "I WANT YOU TO KNOW I'M CREATING A SPACE FOR SOMETHING NEW TO GROW!"

Absolutely calmed by the authority of the voice and wide awake, I immediately responded, "Now that I understand, you can have my house, my practice, my wife, and my children. I relinquish my rights to everything!"

By the end of the week, my caseload was completely full again! With that assurance I continued to see clients and stayed open and in touch with the force of my awakening. From then on, my life required an arduous balancing act between making the day to day decisions required on this side of life while finding a way to cooperate with the dimensions of life beyond the visible and tangible. I constantly longed for a map for the new territory my psyche was exploring.

Here in the Canyon I found myself going through a similar dilemma. I remembered Jung's advice to wait and trust the impersonal power. I expected something to come from that vast resource and rescue me. I wanted magic again. I wanted to be possessed by some mystical motorcycle maestro that would dominate my weary mind and exhausted body. However, nothing showed up and I was all I could find.

A voice deeper than my own kept encouraging me, "Success has to do with trusting the traction available in the unseen. Quit fussing with the handlebars when you steer around the slippery stuff. Drive into the middle of the invisible! Find the certainty there rather than slide around on the loose footing of what you can see." In psychological terms, steering the bike around the slick edges is equivalent to trusting the limited perspective of one's ego. I resonated with Jung's invitation to understand that there is a force behind our psyche's momentum that is carrying our lives in its direction, so the ego's urge to micromanage our lives must be balanced with yielding to the internal GPS that will direct us to where we ought to go. The momentum we were born with will take us to the fulfillment of our lives.

Developing riding skills and consciousness depends on the ability to ride off the edge of the current map to land in new territory and adapt to what we find there. We won't find the world in our maps, our books, or our ideas.

Even though I was totally exhausted by this time of the day, I led the way down a steep incline and, with a fair bit of newly acquired confidence, crossed a foot-deep stream with little difficulty. I spun my way up the other side of the ravine on wet tires. Steam was still rolling off my hot engine that had just taken a dip in the water when I paused to see if the others managed the tricky river crossing. No Tom! No Jake! No engine noise. I turned off my motor and waited for a few moments. "Oh God!" I groaned. The last thing on earth I wanted to do was drive back down the angled and slippery road coming out of the stream. After waiting long enough to figure something bad had happened, I nursed my bike back down the hill and cringed when I saw Tom's black BMW sprawled on its side in the red clay on the other side of the stream. I parked my bike on the edge of the muddy streambed.

"Are you OK?" I asked a stumbling and cursing Tom after I waded across the creek.

"Yeah," he responded with some embarrassment in his voice. "I don't know what happened!" Rubbing his shoulder and his knee, he walked around the downed BMW like a buzzard circling its prey trying to figure out if it was dead or alive. "The tires were squirrelly coming down the hill. The front tire washed out, and splat I was down."

I didn't need an explanation. Dropping the bike there didn't surprise me. That particular section of road had taken on a strange texture. Rather than rock, dirt, sand, or that awful deep red flour dust, the surface was like Teflon. Tractionless. Gummy. Almost greasy, just like my aunt's seasoned iron skillet. Tom looked extremely tired.

Back on the hill Jake motioned to us, "Come on, let's get this thing on its feet."

He crammed his muscular arms underneath the tank, and Tom and I joined him on the side, "One, two, three, HEAVE!" Our tired mantra again united us and we threw our weight against the bike. Both Tom's and my boots slipped on the greasy road, but Jake was able to pick up that big machine by himself. His strength and determination increased my admiration of him, "Thank God you're here!" I panted.

Not one to take in accolades, chest heaving, he narrowed his eyes and flashed at Tom, "OK, now, get your ass on the bike! Gas it and go through the water in the middle of the tracks!"

His look was fierce enough to scare the bike across the creek without a rider. Tom got on and crossed the stream with little difficulty.

I waded back across to my bike and my boots again filled with water. We paused as we always did whenever one of us had an unplanned get-off. It was hard to admit out loud that we'd crashed again, but like a stunned bird that quivers after it hits a window before it flies off again, the shock of hitting the ground hurt, and it took time to flush the adrenalin and mount up again. The three of us, caked head to toe with red mud, sloshing in our sodden boots, stood our bikes on the kickstands to gather ourselves and take a water break.

Ever since we left the asphalt, the trip had been horrible. Just keeping the bike upright required all of my attention, and our hurry and fear kept us from looking at the beauty of the forests we'd been riding through. It was a relief to take my eyes off the road and begin to absorb the scenery around us. We parked near a crumbling stone and mortar shack. Three or four houses, several chickens, goats, and a broken down truck or two dotted the flat where the stream widened and was being diverted to water the garden. This was typical of the many settlements we'd driven through that popped up like termite mounds on small sections of flat land. Some of these villages had Mexican names painted on a board stuck on a post; sometimes the names would even correspond to the scribbles on our crumpled map. This one had no name so we couldn't assure ourselves that we were on the road to Morelos.

Three small boys, aged around five to eight, sat above the creek on a crumbling red stone retaining wall staring at the scene in front of them. They seemed shell-shocked as they looked at three alien men dressed in flaming fluorescent riding gear, wearing full-face helmets, riding heavily loaded motorcycles, muttering in a strange language on the bank of the streambed beneath their front yard.

We nodded in their direction and waved, "Hola." But they just sat motionless with eyes wide open, slowly chewing gum. Staring. Shocked? Scared? Bored? I couldn't tell. We were lost, scared, hungry, tired, and in a rush to find something familiar. They, on the other hand, like seagulls in a gale, oblivious to danger, were safe on their wall, at home.

After a short break to drink some water and drain out my boots, we mounted to pull away. I hadn't even moved my bike when Tom stopped again. "My brakes are acting up again. It feels weird. Can you guys help?"

Not Again! We got off the bikes and when we looked closer we discovered that his rear tire was tortilla flat! No wonder he'd dropped his bike. I ground my teeth, silent in my fury. *I told you to buy a new tire when we were in Guadalajara, and now you've messed up the trip because of your stubborn refusal!* I didn't say it out loud but I wanted to bitch slap him in the worst way.

Tom kicked his tire, threw down his gloves, and his eyes went dark. Another dreaded delay! Our patience was already less than threadbare because of a sleepless night, slimy roads, physical exhaustion, and constant fear. Most difficult for me was the persistent anxiety that we didn't really know where we were or have any idea how to get out. By now all of us were impatient to get to that little dot on our map, Morelos, our fantasy destination for the evening that would surely offer a Motel 6 with a hot shower, gourmet food, and a comfortable bed.

Oh, the curses that filled that streambed as we stormed around! If we had a gun we would have shot that blasted Beemer and thrown it down a cliff. Now the kids saw a real spectacle. They continued watching us like they were animals in a zoo looking at the humans making silly faces against the glass. We took off our riding gear and started looking for the hole in that muddy flat. We all figured that a stone had probably cut through the thin treads. Before we even found the hole Tom groaned, "How do you repair a gash in a tire out here?"

No one spoke. In order to lift the rear tire out of the mud to inspect it, we had to put a rock under the kickstand, then two of us tipped the bike over far enough to lift the rear tire off the ground while the third knelt in the mud, slowly rotating the tire to find the puncture. We all tried our luck locating the hole so we could insert a rubber plug to patch it. When I couldn't see any damage, I shut my eyes and carefully rubbed my fingers over every inch, searching for abnormalities in the tire as if I were reading a Braille text. Nothing.

It spoke to our exhaustion and mental impairment that we didn't even think to pull out one of our portable compressors and fill the flat with air to find where the air escaped. Instead we just kept spinning the tire around and around and around, trying in vain to find the slit or an imbedded stone.

The three of us, now sweating and cursing, frustrated that we couldn't find the puncture but too intelligent to kick the damn thing into the creek, paused to figure out what to do. The irony struck as these kids, calm as the sunrise, watched three frenetic, oddly colored men scramble in the creek bed. We fell into hysterical laughter, imagining what a sight it must be for three shy kids staring at the spectacle unfolding in front of them. "Do you suppose this is their first contact with the outside world? Do you suppose this is all they know of gringos?" I asked.

"What a way to remember gringos." Tom chuckled.

All the time we were looking for the leak, I kept a secret emergency Fix-a-Flat-in-a-Can buried in my saddlebags. I didn't want to give it up, saving it for my own security when I'd be riding home alone. Eventually I offered it as a solution. It was our last resort. The kit included an aerosol can and a clear tube that screws onto the tire's valve stem. Instructions say to hold the can upright and press the button. The pressurized can forces green slime into the tire and then inflates it with air. The instructions read, "After emptying the contents of the can, immediately drive the car for two to four miles and find a gas station and fill your tire with the proper amount of air pressure. *Do not use on motorcycles, bicycles, or high performance tires.*" But it was all we had. The slime is forced into the hole in the tire but as soon as the tire is filled, the rider must drive away as fast as possible so the centrifugal force presses the goo into the leak. If we got Tom moving before all the air escaped, it would work. We hoped. But speed in this section of road was not easy to come by. Could he maintain enough speed to seal the puncture?

Jake, again with utmost urgency in his voice, insisted, "Tom, immediately when we get this thing filled up, ride like hell so the air doesn't escape. Don't stop!" Sometimes the harshness of Jake's tone set our teeth on edge, but this time the urgency overcame the delivery. We all knew at some very important level that if we couldn't repair the tire, this trip would slow down again and we would lose our race against the coming rain.

We all repacked our bikes and got ready to go. Tom, with eyes wide in fear, put on his riding gear, swung his ailing leg over the seat and fired it up. I held the can like an "IV" dripping liquid salvation and watched as the last bubble of green goo slid down the tube and inflated the tire. I quickly unscrewed the can from his valve stem.

Jake slapped the rump of Tom's bike, "Go! Go! Go!"

Tom tore off like death itself was chasing him. Jake and I watched him go. We turned to look at the immobile kids and waved goodbye, glad to be leaving the creek. We exchanged a very serious glance, shrugged our shoulders, and in unison we said, "God, I hope it works." Neither of us wanted to imagine the alternative.

Thirty minutes later everything changed again.

••

What Really Broke

There's no coming to consciousness without pain.   —CG. Jung

Trained motorcyclists know that by staying leaned over in the corner, especially when fear strikes, the traction on a motorcycle will carry them through. They know that fear, not loss of traction, causes wrecks. Likewise humans, when dragged through life's difficult circumstances, learn that there are vast resources in the psyche that will come to their aid and produce growth never thought possible. Life invites us to find that undergirding intelligence and learn to trust it rather than rely on the crude reptilian instincts of survival. Finding what supports us when we can no longer support ourselves is the highest and best experience we can have. I kept appealing to those deeper parts of the psyche, thinking that if I could focus my attention in the right places, I might find a way to be delivered.

It had taken quite a long time to fix Tom's flat, and walking around, stretching, drinking some water allowed me to begin to think more clearly. Our bikes had been taking a serious beating on the rocks. Tom's bike was beginning to rattle apart. He'd already broken the bracket that held on one of his saddlebags. I didn't have any confidence that his tire would hold up. I reasoned it went flat because a stone damaged it and the repair could only be temporary at best. I expected to see his crippled bike whimpering around the next bend. I worried about suspension parts breaking. My eyes were raging-red from all the dust and grit that managed to get under my contact lenses. I didn't like the way Tom was limping on his gimpy hip. It was like we had ridden with such force into a slot canyon that the momentum wedged us between both walls. Even though we were making progress, I knew we had driven so far in that there was no way out. I now began to experience not only the dull ache of fear but also the crushing claws of claustrophobia. I couldn't find the map for continuing on or the map that would lead me out.

Something had to break! This adventure had run its course and I couldn't quiet the internal dialogue that insisted I find a way to stop. I wanted to bail out but I hadn't reached the threshold where an idea becomes a decision. I *wanted* to turn around but was afraid of the fight if I demanded we stop. And then, just like a leak in a dam that quickly becomes a torrent, the pressure in me burst and I made the decision that when I got to Morelos, I was going to abandon ship and find a truck to haul me and my bike back to civilization. I wasn't going to stay!

Something invisible that bound us had just snapped in me. Even though I knew it would be tough for all of us, my loyalty to my own safety overrode my responsibility to stay with Jake and Tom and help them complete their adventure. I'd made my decision, admitted to myself that I didn't have the mettle to go on, and began to shore up some gumption for the sure argument to come.

Tom had followed our advice and aggressively driven away from the tire-changing creek as fast as he could. We hadn't seen him for about thirty minutes when we came to another nasty section. Visible signs of a road disappeared on a deeply crevassed, slanted gypsum rock face. Though dry, the rock was slippery like glass-smooth dry concrete. Every 10 or 15 feet, a 12-inch-deep fissure diagonally crossed the face. They were just wide enough to trap our tires if we didn't hit them with enough speed or sufficient power. Just as when crossing railroad tracks, we had to approach each fracture at least on a 45-degree angle to prevent the tires from dropping into the crevasse. We could see the black residue from truck tires that had spun up the road trying to get enough traction to get to the top.

Midway up the face my front tire fell into one of the angled foot-deep fractures, which immediately pitched the bike in the opposite direction I was going. Like a bull rider catapulted from the high side of a bull's ass, I went flying face first into the rocks at the edge of the road. The motorcycle followed and pinned me to the ground.

My head smashed into some chalky white gypsum stones and I landed hard on a rock. Immediately, searing pain shot through me from my left side. As I lay there gasping, trying to gather myself, I couldn't see much through the dirt caked on my visor. My left leg was trapped under the motorcycle. The motor was still running and the back wheel slowly turned. Everything hurt! I winced when I moved to lift my face shield and gasped in pain when I tried to pull my foot from under the bike. I fumbled to find the key to turn it off.

I didn't want to move. I didn't scream. I clenched my teeth hard, grunted, and heard myself, my resolve clear, "I can't go on! I am finished!"

I rolled onto my back, trying to catch my breath and orient myself. I could hear Jake down below me, struggling to find a level place to put his Beemer on the kickstand. Before he struggled up the hill, two things flashed in my mind, *Oh, shit, I'm in real trouble now!* The second sensation that settled around my physical body was deep relief! *I am relieved because I now have an excuse not to ride any further.* I no longer had to struggle with the decision whether to press on with the ride, or how to rationalize it for Tom and Jake. The damage to my body had made the decision for me. I was not going to ride another inch! My body would not allow it. I'd no idea how or what I would need to do to get back to civilization, but any uncertainty about continuing evaporated.

I reached under my mesh jacket, gingerly touched my ribcage, and found the unmistakable point of icy fire. My breath came in painful gasps. I had broken ribs! I wasn't sure how many. It hurt too much to touch myself. Exhaustion had no doubt played a part in my wreck. Imaginary visions of hurtling over one of the cliffs had been interrupting my concentration all day. Even as I lay there waiting for Jake, I began to wonder if these recurring scenes were premonitions of what was coming or did my persistent imagining of a wreck help create the wreck? A sinister voice accused me, *Because you feel relief even with your pain, maybe that means you made it happen!* The horror of that idea shook me as I was already fending off considerable guilt for having jeopardized our trip.

By the time Jake got to me, I'd managed to get out from under the bike but couldn't yet stand up. He looked down at me, "You OK?"

I winced. "I think I've broken a rib or two."

I was still lying there trying to gather myself when Tom yelled from the top of the hill, "Everything OK?"

"No. Get down here!" Jake called.

Tom shook his head, "No way I'm riding back down that shit! Is Dave all right?"

"No, fuck, he's broken his ribs!" Impatient dismay was thick in Jake's voice. "Where have you been?"

"I parked my bike on a flat section above. I barely made it up and stopped to make sure you guys made it!"

His concern for me was evident but so was his concern for his recently repaired tire. "God, do you think I should still be riding it to make sure my tire is sealed?"

"It ought to be OK by now," Jake hollered back.

I'd been stumbling around trying to catch my breath and worried that it was not good to leave a hot motorcycle on its side in the dirt. Jake was on the same page and said, "Let's get this son of a bitch back on the road." Two and a half men did the one-two-three-heave, pulled it back to the road, scraped off the largest chunks of dirt, and stood it up.

"Tom, Dave and I'll hold it up. Get on and ride this up the hill for him."

"No way, man, you're the better rider, you do it!"

Tom and I held the bike against the gravity of the hill and Jake swung his leg over, pulled in the clutch, and hit the starter. Nothing.

The lights worked, horn worked, fuel injection fired up, but it wouldn't turn over. He tried again. No response.

"How do you start this Goddamn thing?"

"Pull in the clutch, make sure the kickstand is up, make sure the kill switch is in the on position, turn on the key, and hit the starter button."

Nothing. So I tried. Nothing. "Shit shit shit!" A broken body and now a broken bike.

I thought immediately about the wiring/lighting problem I'd been wrestling with before we ever got off the pavement. Just what I feared. Damn it! I should have fixed this problem back in Los Mochis. I never should have come here without illumination!

The physical denial that comes with shock took over and I told them, "You guys take this down the hill a ways so I can figure out how to get it going again."

Bracing themselves against the gravity of the hill they walked it backwards down to a level spot where it would be easier to tear apart.

Though still dazed, my breath coming in gasps, sore from standing up all day on the foot pegs, I welded my left arm to my ribcage and one-handed I began dismantling all my gear to get to the tools that were buried under the seat. It seemed imperative to get it started again even though I knew that I wouldn't be able to ride. I had a full set of tools stashed somewhere but was so stressed, in shock, and feeling the pressure to get moving again that I couldn't find them. Frustrated by my ineptitude, Jake unpacked his own side cases and pulled out his tools. I pulled off my seat, opened the fuse box, and meticulously checked all fuses, connections, and wiring, but I found nothing amiss.

"Maybe it's in the side stand switch. I could have broken that when I went down."

Motorcycles won't start with the kickstand down and it's one of the many reasons a bike won't start. I fixated on memories of several bikes in our motorcycle safety training fleet that wouldn't start because of a broken kickstand switch. So Jake and I, on our knees, took off the switch but could find nothing wrong and put it back on.

I was the most mechanically skilled of the three of us and it was my bike and my responsibility. Nevertheless, I wanted so much for one of them to jump in and rescue me from this problem. All I wanted to do was lie down and rest. This was a worst-case scenario. I hated being broken down, especially out here, of all places, lost, hungry, wounded, out of ideas, and in a country whose language I couldn't understand. I hated that Tom and Jake were hovering over me, unable to make any concrete suggestions. They were not tapping their feet in impatience but the burden of my being broken was a weight that can't be measured on a scale. I wanted to hear some words that told me that they were here with me for the long haul and to take as much time as I needed to sort it out. Our "fuck it" mantra wouldn't work here. I hoped they wouldn't just leave me for the vultures to devour.

Eventually Tom asked out loud to no one, "What are our options?"

We all decided that our only option was to flag down the next truck and see if I could hitch a ride to Morelos.

"Yeah, if we can get you a ride, Tom and I can meet you there." There was no assurance in Jake's voice but a decision had been made that allowed us to focus beyond what was here. "We gotta be careful though. Some of those men in the 4x4's scared the shit out of me."

A somber silence washed over us as we sat waiting on the edge of the road. I didn't know what was going through their minds. We didn't talk much. Within a half hour, we heard the growl of a vehicle coming up the hill. A dirty green Jeep SUV pulled up with four men inside. They just stared at us, evaluating something, and with coldness in their eyes asked, *"¿Está bien?"* My hackles jumped to attention.

"Sí, no problema," we all chimed in unison, feeling without

talking to each other that it would be imprudent to let them know how desperate we were. As they drove off, the hackles on my neck went back to normal. Fifteen minutes later we heard another truck laboring up the hill, crawling over rocks in first gear.

"God, I hope this truck doesn't raise the hair on the back of my neck," I managed through clenched teeth, hoping it was not one of those fancy dark-windowed trucks filled with men talking on their ritzy two-way radios. Because little is written about this uncharted territory, I'd no idea how much drug production and drug traffic thrived here. Only after returning did I begin to understand that the entire area was overrun with the activity of the drug cartels. Sitting there with pain in my ribs and time to reflect, it sank in on me what an awful situation we were in. I was relieved not to be sitting on my motorcycle seat but beyond that, I knew I was in trouble.

"Yeah, we could be fucked." Tom nodded his head.

While we were riding we assumed that we could always outrun danger, but weakened, stationary, and incapacitated, my dread got worse. Jake had shown us his Taser and I never asked but assumed that he was also packing some other weapons to protect himself. He had been in many physical altercations during his gang days and his capacity to exude intimidating physical presence allowed me to proceed on this adventure feeling safer than had I gone with a more timid soul.

The next pickup that labored up the hill was a jacked-up Ford 150 club cab. A young man stuck his head out the window and asked us, *"Es bueno?"* This time instead of *"Gracias, estamos bien,"* we waved them over and in our broken Spanish we managed the words *"moto accidente, infermo"* (sick) and Tom, who had become our default translator, picked up a stick and broke it and pointed to my rib, *"¿Costilla?"*

I exaggerated my suffering just a bit, and their eyes lit up in understanding. They repeated, *"costilla rota"* (broken rib) and the mystery of why three gringos were sitting on the side of the road next to their motorcycles finally made sense to them.

Struggling with a few words of Spanish and sign language gave way to looks of compassion. I pointed to my motorcycle and said, *"Moto no está bien."*

"¿Ésta es la calle a Morelos?" Tom asked, and they nodded. This was indeed the road to Morelos.

By this time the driver had come around to our side and was now the one speaking to us. They got it that I had a broken rib, was very weak and sore, and we asked them if we could load the bike into the truck and would they take me to Morelos.

While we were talking I was comforted and dismayed at the same time. Though relieved that the pickup was filled with a family, not drug runners, my hope faded as I watched nine people pour out of the cab to check us out. I feared there was not enough room for the bike and me. It would be better than walking, but I imagined that if they'd take me, I'd probably spend the trip bouncing around in the pickup bed with my bike.

Three of the men put their heads together and after a brief debate flashed us big smiles, nodding their heads to indicate they would take both me and my bike to Morelos. I'd lucked my way into finding a man taking his family all the way to the town I'd been dreaming about.

After scouting the immediate area, and much jabbering, gesturing, and suggestions from the three of us, the driver found a level place and backed down the road to a ditch so we wouldn't have to lift the bike four feet off the ground into the bed of the pickup. We horsed it into the truck, put as much of my gear as possible under it to cushion it and tied it down. With my gear, my bike, and their things in the back, and with a Mariachi band booming from an MP3 player, the driver insisted that I sit up front with him and his companion.

I relaxed a bit at the warmth in their generous smiles but had a fair bit of terror at leaving the safety Jake, Tom, and I had created. It's not that I loved Tom and Jake but we were bound because we survived together. Before I crammed myself onto the hard center console with my head pressed sidewise against the roof, I looked at Tom and Jake, who had begun to repack their bikes. "Well, here's hoping we all get to Morelos. Let's try to find each other when we get there." My relief was evident. I didn't envy the rest of the trip for them. I had no idea how long they would have to ride, how big Morelos was, nor did I have any idea how we would ever connect again.

Another dam had burst. Without any real hope of seeing them again, a sappy "see you later" accompanied our lingering handshakes. Something invisible evaporated when we parted. I began the next phase of my journey, not knowing if I was descending deeper or being lifted out of this hell.

••

Don't Drink the Water!

What is the hardest task in the world? To think.

—Ralph Waldo Emerson

The three of us had scratched and clawed our way to a hard-won togetherness in the week since we had left Ajijic. Though we'd started out with only our love of nature and motorcycle riding to bind us, the stress, fear, and actual danger had amalgamated us into a strong camaraderie. Our mutual dependency was not a harmonious marriage but a necessary one, a paradoxical one, boxed by Jake's tenacity, Tom's long-term loyalty to Jake, and a shared commitment to survival as we traveled deeper into the unknown. In our desire to make it to Mexico's famed Copper Canyon we traveled so far that I didn't know if we'd ever get there or get back. I'd sacrificed my desire to abandon the quest for the sake of keeping cohesion in the group. I had mistaken Jake's bull-headed confidence for competence as a leader.

Our unity had started to collapse as we sat there waiting for me to find a way to Morelos. The weak handshake when we parted alarmed me. The alignment of our relationships now again dramatically shifted as Jake and Tom solidified their resolve to make it without me. The cords that once bound us became gossamer memories as soon as I stepped into the cab of the truck and was driven off. I was alone, now on the outside of what I used to be inside.

I was in a four-wheeled vehicle that wouldn't tip over if it hit a rock, would not drop me into a sink hole, and best of all, I didn't have to keep standing up on the bucking foot pegs, using my legs to absorb the shock of the rugged road. And it had music. Not my kind of music, but a kind of music that let me experience the fierce independence of Mexicans scratching out an existence in an inaccessible land that few outsiders ever visit. While I experienced every jarring bump in relative safety, my former partners rode tired and hungry with many hours of uncertainty in front of them. Even though I was not sure where I was being taken, riding with natives gave me some assurance that we were going somewhere.

In the truck, none of them spoke a word of English. *"¿Cómo se llama?"* I asked the young man driving.

"Me llamo Enrique."

"My name is David." We shook hands and I introduced myself to the rest of the family and immediately forgot all their names. Four generations stuffed themselves without murmur or complaint in the back seat. The great grandfather, wearing a brilliant white cowboy hat he never removed, sat behind the passenger seat. On his lap perched a smiling five-year-old girl, quiet as if she had been instructed not to speak. A young mother pressed next to him, holding her year-old infant boy, who complained only when it was time to nurse. An older woman, obviously the matron of the group, sat with a three-year-old crawling all over her. A silent teenage girl spent the entire trip with earphones plugged into her ears, picking at her fingernails.

No longer bouncing up and down on the bike, I was now being tossed side to side as the F-150 jostled from washout to rock, in and out of ruts. I winced each time the cab slammed back and forth. Whenever the cab rocked harder than usual Enrique looked at me and cringed as if he was feeling my pain. He could have driven faster but instead drove as gently as he could, making sure my bike wasn't being damaged in the back. The passenger on my right had his eyes glued in the mirror and several times we stopped to tighten my bright orange Home Depot tie-down straps and their brown overused hemp ropes. We'd traveled for about an hour and at a fork in the road turned to our right, stopping 100 yards later at a stone house. Before we got out, I attempted to assure myself that we were still going where I thought we were. "Is this the road to Morelos?" I asked in my broken Spanish, pointing down the road straight ahead.

"No, otro." Enrique pointed back down the road 100 yards to

the other road in the fork. He went inside and shortly came out with the man of the house. They both slid on their backs under the truck with a rusty pair of vise grips and began working on the drive train.

I bent over to get a better look at what they were doing, "*¿Qúe pasa?*"

They seemed grateful that I'd shown genuine interest and they spoke rapidly, pointing to the front universal joint. I understood the international language of mechanical breakdown and immediately knew that the u-joint was loose and beginning to fail. They also showed me the leaking seal at the back of the transmission and I then figured that the growling I'd heard from inside the truck was the metal-on-metal grinding of a deteriorating bearing.

This ancient mechanical problem-solving brotherhood left me with warmth that reminded me of working with my uncle on his ranch the summer my father died. We'd often convene at the local hardware store with other men to solve a new mechanical problem. We didn't call it a "Mexican workaround" then, but I'd begun to use that phrase after my brief time in Mexico. I liked the way the Mexican men used the same communal approach to figure out how to repair nearly everything.

Satisfied for the time being, they rolled out from under the truck, slapped it on its rump, winked at me, and said, "*Está bien.*" I smiled back, wondering if this same kind of mechanical ingenuity could work around what I assumed to be a sophisticated electrical problem in the bowels of my bike's computer?

As Enrique walked to the little junk food store to buy some soda for his family, I heard Jake and Tom toiling up the road behind us. I stepped onto the road, hoping to tell them they'd taken the wrong road. Like bloodhounds they'd been following the tracks of the truck, but I groaned when they waved and roared past. I furiously waved them back with my working arm. Fortunately Tom saw me and turned around. Over the din of his motor, I yelled, "You're going the wrong way. Morelos is that way." I looked at the family to make sure I had it right. They nodded.

Tom flipped up his visor, "How ya holding up?"

"I'm really sore, but it's sure better than riding!"

"OK, catch you later." The concern in his face was not directed to me. He was exhausted and focused on his own safety.

Impatient to get on their way, they waved me a weary goodbye and sent rooster tails of dirt behind them as they tore off. With them in front, I could at least follow their tracks in the dirt and if they dropped a bike or needed directions, we could help. Now that I was riding "sweep" I could hold up my responsibility for their safety a little bit, but I couldn't help them if they took a wrong turn.

I wanted to express my gratitude to the family for their willingness to accommodate the additional burden I'd become to their trip. I reached into my tank bag in the bed and found my last Snickers bar. Before we took off again, I turned to the mother in the back seat, *"Muchas gracias, muchas, muchas gracias,"* and offered them my last bit of food.

Dazed, half-dozing in the confines of the truck, dulled by the constant beat of the music, I had time to think about all that had happened in the last few days. With curiosity and judgment I asked myself why I'd experienced so much relief when I wrecked. I was disturbed by my inner accuser that blamed me for "causing" the wreck, and by my passivity for not insisting that we return before someone got hurt.

I dove into the troubling questions. Did I bring on this accident to give myself a way out? Did I need a broken bone for an excuse to exit from the ordeal that was causing so much fear? Did my unconscious mind create a relatively small trauma to protect me from a more severe accident later on?

The patter of guilt from a popular notion haunted me. It says there is a reason for every traumatic event that happens. This implies that nothing is a mistake and our task is to discover the reason for the trauma. Most often the implication is that the individual has a necessary life lesson that he cannot learn otherwise. Furthermore, we create these sufferings for that purpose. Various empty platitudes accompany this philosophy: "this is your Karma" or "you choose your life circumstances" or "we create our own reality" or "you manifest whatever you focus on," etc. All of these stem from the idea that everything we experience is caused by something. It is the old religious belief that an omnipotent God makes everything happen.

That niggling prosecutor was still alive in me accusing me of causing my wreck and my injury in order avoid a fight with Jake and Tom. I still carried a psychological sore spot from a particularly devastating wound the day Dad died. Immediately after my aunt told me the sad news, I ran to my bedroom and cried, pounded my fist against the bed and screamed, "Why, why, why?" My aunt called the minister from the local Baptist church to help answer my questions and calm me down. He came in, sat beside me on the edge of the bed. True to his fundamentalist Christian beliefs, he told me that God was in control of everything, this was God's will and He had obviously "taken my father home." In the practiced phrases of a man hiding behind theology, he looked me in the eye, "This was all part of God's plan. For you to spend the afternoon crying over your loss means that you're questioning God's wisdom. Since your father is in heaven with Jesus, why in the world would you cry? Remember, all things work together for good…" He tossed a few Bible verses at me and walked away believing he'd fulfilled his pastoral duty because I was no longer in doubt and screaming at God.

I didn't have an intellectual basis to revolt against his theology. Dutiful to the Christianity I'd grown up in, I cauterized the gusher of my grief and didn't cry again. Not then, not on the bus ride back to Oregon, not even at the funeral.

Ten years later, after I'd struggled as an emotional orphan through high school, living with a frigid stepmother, making it through college and working on my master's thesis in graduate school, all my long-suppressed grief and rage finally burst to the surface. The doctrine that God in His infinite wisdom purposefully "took my parents home to heaven" for my better good had served like the plug of a volcano. I erupted when it dawned on me that fundamentalist theology at its root is designed to stifle and repress the real emotions that come with life. I'd spent years condemning myself because I had so much emotion roiling inside. I'd driven a wedge of denial between what my body sensed and what I'd allowed into my consciousness, and in so doing spread an immense stain of guilt across my whole personality. When I stifled my heartache and replaced my doubts and anger with a mask of spirituality, the church applauded me for being strong and admired me for being faithful. However, even though I managed to "keep the faith," the grief never diminished and turned me sour inside. My allegiance to the theology simply turned me into a liar.

It was a bit strange to me that I was riding in untamed Mexico with strangers I'd never see again, nursing a broken rib and broken motorcycle, thinking about Dad's death, fundamentalism, and why things happen as they do. Why, while rattling through this Canyon, broken, lost, with little ability to communicate with my riding companions, was I chewing on this old psychological wound? My dad, his death, and the love my brother and I had for motorcycling were all working in the background. Afraid I'd never get out of this situation alive, I was in a ripe place to explore my vulnerabilities. Like a dog that keeps licking its wound, I returned to my reflections.

It had taken years for me to disengage from an arrogant fundamentalist milieu in which every thought, feeling, fantasy, or behavior had to be categorized as either good or evil, right or wrong. Even though the Christian theology I grew up in turned out to be an intellectual mess, I watched over the years as major parts of our Western culture relaxed some of its dogmatism and became gradually more tolerant of liberal issues that were not acceptable in the 50's and 60's. Fewer and fewer Christians accepted that an all-powerful God manipulates good or bad events to achieve His will. Cultural assumptions shifted, values loosened, and support for more individual freedom increasingly gave new shape and texture to our cultural values.

However, vestiges of that one-sided theology still seeped into the collective consciousness of modern thinking as well. Whereas it became out of fashion to easily call all tragedy God's will, the new guiding ethic shifted focus and implied that individuals *create* or *choose* their life circumstances. Somehow in the unconscious machinations, individuals were responsible for what came to them in life. In medical circles, pop psychology, modern religious expressions, abuse, and diagnosis of diseases, the accusing question became, "What did you do to bring on this particular issue that is causing you pain?" Too many have heard some simplistic explanation that they brought on their cancer or that an illness was caused by an unresolved personal problem. The pernicious idea that something, some force, a repressed emotion, or some error in living had to be the cause of personal trauma still lurks around.

Even though the experience of the heron's death collapsed my shallow notion that every event has a discernible cause, the idea that I was responsible for my wreck in order to get out of my dilemma haunted me like a ghost that I'd not completely exorcised. I could almost taste the idea that I'd caused my wreck to learn a lesson. I hated that I was still haunted by the noxious theology that wanted to take another bite out of me. I'd already seen how its poison did nothing more than numb my capacity to feel. It seems that mystery is an ambiguity humans cannot tolerate and therefore they cling to belief systems that relieve them of living with the unknown.

I'd intellectually settled this years ago. We don't create our adversities nor is there a divine, omnipotent force that sets up trauma to teach us things for our good. Just because we learn from life's mistakes does not imply we create the mistakes to learn something. That would mean that a sinister divine force creates all the starvation, war, and suffering in the world. I'd grown past the superstitious need to find a divine force to blame. Just because times of emergency have always offered opportunity to deepen community and develop individual skills cannot mean that some superhuman force designed calamities for this purpose. Shit happens. No, I didn't unconsciously bring on the wreck to bail me out, but I still had to face the task of finding a way out. No one else was going to do that.

I remembered a line from a poem I'd turned into a prayer and dedication to myself, *Attend me, hold me in your muscular flowering arms, protect me from throwing any part of myself away.* It appeared to me now that abandoning my own feelings to continue with our riding group awakened the painful memory of denying my truth after Dad died. I had turned away from myself hoping to find safety in the three of us riding as a group. Though it was understandable that I'd made a choice to be here, I had to live with the equal and opposing truth: I said *no* to my inner wisdom by not turning back sooner. Betrayal to myself was the thread that tied it all together.

Then it struck me. By spending the time traveling, mulling over the problem of causation, I'd fallen into the trap that I'd spent years in my psychotherapy practice helping clients overcome. I'd been teaching them how to enter the stillness at the center of their being so they could participate in the vitality of what was happening in the moment. I'd learned how to help them drop away from mental distraction and experience the fullness of the here and now. In my weakened state, where conscious awareness would have nourished me, my mind was off fussing with ideas of causation and blame. I'd lost control and was traveling unaware through some of the most beautiful country in the world! My thinking kept me from attending to what was here. I'd been ignoring a unique opportunity to engage with and learn from this silent Tarahumara family. Maybe now I could return my attention to the beauty that surrounded me and absorb something from the deep interiority of my new travel mates.

Enrique had just finished descending another steep down-hill, crossed a washout, and nursed his truck back up the other side. As if in sync with my resolve to head out of my navel-gaz-ing and participate in the ride, he stopped his truck and shut off the engine. I looked at the road and could still see two sets of motorcycle tire tracks. Tom and Jake were still on the right road. When Enrique motioned for me to get out, another surge of adrenalin shot through me. Both he and the man in the pas-senger seat stood in front of the truck, insisting that I get out. Defenseless and with my jack-hammering heart pounding, I extricated myself from my perch on the center console. Every time I contracted my abs, icicles of pain shot from my side. The hackles on the back of my neck jumped to attention and tremors of fear shot up and down my spine. Was this the place where they would push me off the cliff, steal my bike, and leave me to die?

He walked me over to the edge of the cliff and pointed to a demolished truck 750 feet below. He lifted his eyebrows, *"Muy peligroso."* This was the second truck I'd seen today that had plunged off the edge. I couldn't imagine the courage it took to drive these narrow roads in a dump truck.

"Comprendo," I nodded. Of course I understood the danger. In my imagination I'd tumbled down one of these steep cliffs a hundred times. His pointing out the wreck only heightened my awareness of the risky territory we'd been traveling and the relief that Enrique was driving and not me.

He then turned to his right, looked out over the view, and spread out his arms in a grand gesture. Stretched before us was a particularly beautiful valley. He reached into the cab, turned off his music to experience the silence. We all basked in the splendor of this valley filled with V-shaped canyons and ridg-es that seemed symmetrically stacked all the way to the sky. These V's stretched as far as we could see. It was as rugged and green as any rainforest.

"*Es muy bonita, muy, muy bonita.*" I was stunned!

Their wonder in the face of nature's beauty was identical to mine and they swelled in pride that this dirty mud-caked white guy swooned at the beauty below. We belonged to the same misty-eyed tribe. I walked back to the truck and found my camera and immediately regretted that I'd not taken more time to capture the magnificence of these mountains before I crashed.

After returning to the cab, I thought what a waste fear is! When I *imagined* that they were going to push me over the cliff my body immediately went into adrenalin-shrieking trauma, my visual focus narrowed, and my instinct to fight or flee kicked in *as if I were in danger*. However, Enrique simply wanted to share Beauty with me!

I wanted relief. I conjured a hot shower, some food, and a comfortable bed when we got to Morelos, but that didn't help the sting that ripped through my body every time the truck rolled from side to side. I had a crick in my neck from being crammed sideways against the roof of the truck and I was falling deeper into shock. All I wanted to do was sleep.

Another opportunity to get out and stretch came when Enrique stopped at a small farm an hour later. A well-kept house with a modest yard was up to my right, and a barn with some horses, goats, and chickens to the left. I was struck buy the cleanliness of this place—no trash, an actual gate, and no auto carcasses rotting on the property. Several children ran up to the truck to see who had stopped by. Enrique got out and talked briefly with the farmer who went to the barn and returned with a 20-foot section of rope. The motorcycle had worked loose and they needed another rope to get it tied right. One of the guys crawled under the truck to find a better place to tie it off. They repositioned the spare tire and some of the junk in the back of the bed and retightened the straps and ropes we already had. Four men grabbed the bike, shook it, tweaked it some more and motioned for me to test it as well. We nodded to each other, *Está bien*. The bike was now safe to travel again. They didn't ask for a deposit to make sure the rope found its way back.

Just before we pulled away, the woman of the house, wearing a long skirt and white blouse, her hair pulled back with a colorful barrette, walked towards us. She looked softly into my eyes, wrapped her warm brown hands around mine, and offered two pills that she had taken out of their wrapping. The glass of water she offered was crystal clear and she indicated that these pills would help with the pain. I remembered the mantra drilled into us ever since we came to Mexico, DON'T DRINK THE WATER! I imagined the horror stories of Montezuma's revenge, dysentery, and the dreaded parasites that have made so many gringos deathly ill.

Caught again between an inner voice that said *you will suffer for this* and the genuineness of this *señora's* hospitality, the kindness of her eyes won out and I guzzled the entire glass of water, savoring its mountain-spring freshness like a man who hadn't drunk a drop in days. She gave me six extra pills to tuck in my pocket and I made sure I could read the label in case I needed to buy more. In just a few minutes the pain tablets kicked in, and for the first time in hours I began to feel relief. The thought of getting sick because of the water never crossed my mind again. I don't know when I'd ever experienced such grace.

An hour later Enrique tapped my leg and pointed across a wide valley to some buildings on the other side. A canyon-wide smile beamed across his face, "*¡Morelos, allá Morelos!*" Within forty-five minutes we'd worked our way down to the river. It was growing dark when we crossed it and entered a very tiny, desolate Mexican village. This was not the Morelos I had in mind at all. I seriously wondered if any foreigners had ever visited this town.

••

More or Less Moral-less in Morelos

How we squander our hours of pain!
How we gaze beyond them into the bitter duration
to see if there is an end...

—Rainer Maria Rilke

Morelos had become for me a magic crystal, the skin of a living hope, the X on a treasure map, a fantasy for salvation. However, the minute we had forded the river and climbed the opposite bank, my vision and hope of an actual town, with streets, sidewalks, stores and restaurants, maybe even a hotel, completely vanished. My head banged against the roof one more time as we bounced across a deeply rutted main street. The sun, like my internal reserves, had disappeared below the mountains, and only a dusky light illuminated the streets. I was too weary to groan.

Enrique stopped on a rise and everyone got out of the truck and was greeted with hugs and kisses by a family group that poured out of a small adobe house. The men of the family all came to the bed of the pickup to look at the *moto* and stare at the grungy man perched on the center console. I stepped out onto the dirt and shook hands with a few of them. I then realized that the family in Enrique's truck was not his family. He served as a sort of taxi service to take the indigenous from the remote areas to the "big city" of Morelos. The family emptied the truck of their sparse luggage, diaper bags, some food, and miscellaneous personal belongings. Enrique and I, now alone in the truck, continued up the hill. I finally had a regular seat to sit on.

"Te quiero!" "I want you!" Enrique, a very handsome young man, whistled his howling wolf to a young woman walking up the road. She blushed and dropped her head, faking embarrassment in what seemed to be a well-practiced courtship ritual.

Driving away from the center of town he stopped several vehicles and talked to various men on the street. I heard his query, *"¿Mecánico a moto?"* I understood that he was looking for a motorcycle mechanic. He finally got some directions, nodded his head, and drove to a house near the edge of town. He paused on the street, with motor still running, and whistled shrilly before a home on the right. The house was a small, tin-roofed brick structure on an embankment four feet above the road. A crude stone wall protected it from the torrents of rainwater that rushed down the road past his home and through the middle of town. The moist soil and puddles gave evidence of recent rain. A portly man in his late forties answered Enrique's hail and they conversed for a few minutes. Then Enrique, all smiles, indicated to me that he had found a mechanic and that we could drop the bike off here.

I looked at the barrel-chested, thick mustached Mexican man wearing a greasy grey tee shirt. His clear eyes met mine as I extended my hand to shake the hambone-sturdiness of his gnarled and oily hand, the hand of a hard-working and honest man. It was like shaking hands with a hardened mesquite log. *"Hola, mi nombre es David."*

"Are you a mechanic?" I asked. "A motorcycle mechanic? I have an electrical problem, can you help me?" I was fishing for hope, and my garbled Spanish, my sophisticated hand gestures, and accompanying motorcycle sounds only approximated my trouble.

His hesitation concerned me. He shrugged his shoulders, opening his hands in a gesture of uncertainty, *"más o menos."* I'd hoped for a robust, *"Sí, Señor"* but because Mexicans feel it's impolite to refuse a request, they won't admit that they can't do whatever you ask. I had absolutely no faith that he understood more about a motorcycle's electrical system than I did.

I had no choice, the night was here and as tired, hungry, and sore as I was, I nodded my acquiescence and figured that in the morning I'd come back to problem-solve with him. Enrique backed his truck up against the berm, dropped his tailgate, called on another neighbor to help, and the four of us rolled the bike into the "mechanic's" yard. He offered to store my gear in his house, but I thought it best to pull as much of my gear off as I could carry, afraid that any gear left on the bike might find legs and not be there in the morning. I locked my helmet to the bike, packed all I could into my removable saddlebags, and had Enrique toss it all into the back of the truck.

"I'll be back here at 9:00 in the morning." I looked down and patted Suzi's filthy seat.

In the complete dark, Enrique and I turned back towards the middle of town. A few streetlights and the dim glow from the small homes lining the streets gave meager illumination to the night. He turned left and then right and then left again, and by now I was completely turned around and lost within being lost. I wasn't tracking well and hoped that in the morning I could find my way back up the hill to the outskirts of town to my motorcycle. I figured that I'd be walking.

The town was still alive with kids, joyously running, jumping, singing, and playing with the dogs. The distant murmur of music from a bar not far away filtered through the raucous noise of the kids. All of a sudden Enrique stopped and pointed to the street, *"¡Sus amigos!"*

There on the corner, Jake and Tom sat on a rudimentary concrete foundation with bent angle iron sticking out like dead tree stumps. They saw me at the same time Enrique saw them. They had sodas in their hands and some sort of food they were spooning out of a cup.

"David! David, over here! Damn, you made it! Good to see you!" Jake expressed genuine relief that I'd arrived safely.

Preoccupied with the drama of finding a mechanic, I'd completely forgotten about them. I was astonished to see them. They were just as shocked to see me again. I'd separated so completely from them that I no longer hoped to reconnect. "Man, am I ever glad to see you! Did you guys make it OK?

Where are you staying? Did you find a hotel?" I had a million questions for them. "Is there a hotel? Where is it?"

I wanted them to jump up, come to the truck, and help me. Instead they just sat there and hollered to me, "There is a fat lady wearing a red top who will give you a room. We got a room up there." Tom pointed over his right shoulder with his thumb.

A dozen little children, excited to see another gringo, scurried under my feet as Enrique dropped my gear onto the dusty street. I looked around for the fat woman in the red top who ran the hotel. In Morelos the hotel didn't have a flashing sign in the window or anything else that would indicate a place of business, and no fat woman in a red top! I kept one eye on my gear, now spread on the ground, fearing that the poor people there would view it as free stuff. My other eye scanned the gathering crowd for a red top. Jake and Tom continued to sit on the cement and didn't lift a finger to help.

I turned to Enrique, *"¿Cuánto cuesta?"*

Grateful for his kindness and carefulness to get me out of my predicament, I would have given him whatever he asked. He shrugged his shoulders, turned up his hands in the universal gesture of whatever, *"No sé."* I had the sense that he had not done this for the money; he helped me because that was the decent thing to do. I didn't have much cash and had no idea what it would cost me to fix my bike and get back to civilization. I thought about how much the workers get paid in Ajijic and decided that I would pay him what was more than a good day's wage. I offered him 400 pesos. I felt cheap offering him the equivalent of $30.00 USD. *"Gracias, mi amigo."* Money could never equal my gratitude. We said goodbye and I immediately began to miss him.

In time, the woman who ran the hotel came to the street and motioned me to follow her. I struggled against my pain and fear of being ripped off, gathered my gear in my arms as best I could, and walked through the chaos of the kids in the street. As I struggled past Jake and Tom, my fury got the best of me. "Damn you, motherfuckers! Why don't you help? I come into this strange town at dark with a broken rib and you just sit there on your fat asses and don't help. Fuck you running! You bastards!"

"Hey man, back off. We just got here ourselves and are too tired to move. You've been sitting in a truck all afternoon. Shut the fuck up!" Something like jealousy tinged Tom's rejoinder.

She led me down the hall to one of the rooms, knocked on the door as if someone might have been in there and cried out, "*Hola. Hola.*" She knocked again.

I thought it was creepy that she didn't know which rooms were occupied and which weren't. I wondered if I would be sleeping on sheets that been sullied by a passionate couple that had broken into her keyless room. She tried in vain to open the door and asked me to wait a minute. Soon her twenty-something son came to the room with a handle-less blade of an old serrated knife. His rapped his knuckles against the wood and his strong voice got no response. When no one answered, he shoved the blade between the doorframe and the jamb and began sawing through the nails. Finally he was able to pry them apart, force the knife against the latch, and release it.

The door opened to an 8x8-foot space with two single beds and an air-conditioner in a window frame propped with a rusted piece of angle iron and enough wire to string a fence. A rusted screen with a hole in it the size of a small pumpkin loosely covered the open window. A glaring light bulb lit the barren bathroom. The toilet had no seat, there were no towels, and just one partially used bar of soggy soap in the sink.

I asked the manager if the air-conditioner worked and she nodded, but when she turned it on, nothing happened.

"Please," I prayed out loud.

"*No problema, Señor,*" and she summoned her son again, muttered some Spanish to him and he disappeared.

He came back with a length of old extension cord that had

the male end cut off. He stripped the end of the wires, jammed the bare ends into the wall socket, and turned on the air conditioner. It coughed to life and roared like a 747. Delicious air began to circulate in the stuffy room. The fan worked but no cold air came out of the vents. This would be where I'd spend the night. I had no energy to demand something nicer. I paid her the $18.00 and walked back to the street to talk to Jake and Tom.

Hunched against the old foundation, they hadn't moved. Their heads drooped and they barely had the energy to greet me. "What did you have to pay for the room?" Tom asked as if trying to connect again.

"$250 pesos. What a dive. The air-con doesn't work but at least they got the fan going. The guy stripped the extension cord and just stuffed the ends into the outlet. Don't you love Mexico? But it's a bed. I'll just lather up with mosquito repellent and make the best of it. Where'd you find something to eat?" I turned to Jake.

"The lady in the red top owns a little store down the street. We got some cookies and pop there."

My questions kept coming. "After you guys passed us, I'd see your tracks on the road but lost them a while back. How long have you been here?"

"We both dumped our bikes before we got here. Tom hit some mud and went down again, and once I just lost the front end and went down too." It was rare for Jake to fall and rarer for him to admit it.

"Did you get hurt?"

"Naw." Tom lifted his head from between his shoulders, "We pulled into town about an hour ago. I've never been so tired in all my life! My legs are like jelly."

"I'm sorry about jumping on you guys like that. I'm just at my end."

"Don't worry about it." I think Tom was quite used to being yelled at. "How're ya feeling?"

"My ass is sore from sitting on the center console, my neck aches from bending over the whole trip, and my rib hurts like hell. I am so thankful that I found these guys. There is no way I could have ridden." I wanted to reinforce my pain in case they'd try to talk me out of my determination to call it quits once and for all.

"Where's your bike?"

"We dropped it off in a mechanic's yard somewhere on the other side of town. He doesn't know squat about electronics. I took everything off the bike that I could carry. I told him I'd come back in the morning to work on it. I hope it'll be there. I can't figure anything out now. I'm going to bed and sort things out in the morning. We stopped by a farm and a woman gave me some pills that really helped with the pain. I still have six left. I'm going to drug myself to sleep. See you in the morning."

It never dawned on me to go into my own medicine kit and pull out my own stash of painkillers.

I limped to my room, took a cold shower, dried off with a dirty long-sleeve T-shirt, took some pills, slathered my head and arms with mosquito repellent, and crawled into stained, gritty, threadbare sheets that someone had washed in the sand of the river and forgotten to rinse. The 747 roaring in my ear drowned any street noise and I arranged myself in the most comfortable position I could and dropped into a fitful sleep.

Early in the morning the cacophony of roosters welcoming the first glow of light woke me long before I was ready. Overnight my legs had turned from the rubber of the day before into lactic acid-laced frozen muscles that refused to move. The rest of my body, bruised from the wreck and strained from picking up the bikes from our unplanned get-offs, had stiffened as well. I ached everywhere, like a creaky old man who had been tumbled in a washing machine. It hurt to breathe, and I didn't want to move.

Sleep didn't return. It was the first time I had to consciously assess my situation after my disillusionment with Morelos. The effect of the pain relievers had worn off and the grinding of bone on bone in my ribs let me know that even if I could get my bike running again, I couldn't ride. I was stranded in a village with far fewer resources than I'd imagined.

I came to the conclusion that both the intermittent malfunction of my headlights and the fact that the bike wouldn't start were all from a critical failure in the bike's computer (CPU) that had progressively worsened by the pounding of the roads. I assumed that the flaw was fatal. Because I committed myself to that hypothesis, I also concluded that the local mechanic would not be able to help get it started. Even if he could fix it, the beating my body took in the days previous made riding out impossible. I figured my bike was a goner. I couldn't imagine even riding out in a truck.

Besides my problems, I was here with two friends who were impatient to get on with their journey. I'd become an anchor that was keeping them from getting out. I was sure they would not be willing to wait for me to fix my bike and get physically ready to ride. Most of all, they didn't know that all the time in the truck had solidified my decision to end my trip in Morelos. I wanted to relieve them of their consternation as to what to do with a gimpy rider and a broken bike.

Even though we had reconnected in Morelos, I was alone, now outside the coalition with Jake and Tom. I couldn't get a grip on all my fear. Riding for the last few days in terror of the road seemed to encase me in the paralysis of danger. My ability to speak Spanish was minimal. I'd been in the country for only three months, didn't understand rural Mexican customs, and mistrusted the people and the hostile land. I wanted help, but without language to formulate a plan the fear-mongering part of my brain created more fear and swept me along with it.

I'd worked for years training myself to come into relationship with fear, knowing that resisting fear dramatically makes it worse. I'd seen how relating to fear, even loving it, allowed more advanced aspects of the mind to problem-solve and expand options rather than shut them down. I kept repeating to myself a quote from the Tao de Ching; *"Do you have the patience to wait until the mud settles and the water clears? Can you remain unmoving until the right action arises by itself?"* I was desperate to create a script, any script I could adopt and follow.

The longer I lay there, wanting to shift my body to a more comfortable position but too miserable to move, my desperation grew. I saw no options. My love for my motorcycle and my love for my life had me trapped and these two competing loves were tearing me apart. What I should do with the bike and how to haul it out weighed heavier on me than when my 550-pound motorcycle lay across my body. It didn't occur to me to trust the Mexican people in that humble village.

Then a new thought entered my mind like a sinister seed that began to spread its pernicious roots. Initially I tried to fight off the idea but eventually it caught fire and once I had said it out loud to myself, it repeated itself like a song or a spinning prayer wheel. I tried to dissipate the hope that the new plan cranked up, but it wouldn't leave. The plan told me to abandon my bike, but make an insurance claim that I had wrecked and the bike plummeted into the Canyon. I would say that I hitched a ride out to get medical attention.

I'd developed a new script to follow and my spirit immediately lifted. I began to look at every angle and massage the story. Could I get away with a bald face lie to the insurance company? How would the insurance company ever know? What about the moral implication? Could I live with a lie that large?

This idea took root and became the story of my deliverance. The minute the story took over, something shifted and the idea became a decision, and with that decision all other possibilities vanished.

Buoyed by my new exit strategy, I greeted Jake and Tom in the morning, "I found a place to eat. Just across the street a woman has a couple of tables she uses as a small restaurant. I'm starved. Let's get some food."

I wanted their support for the plan I hatched in the night. I also wanted them to be able to get on with their journey without feeling responsible for my welfare.

Before we walked across the street for breakfast, Jake said, "I've been thinking about your situation all night. You've got insurance right?"

"Yeah."

"Do you have theft on it?"

"Yeah."

"Good. If I were in your shoes, I'd find someone to drive me out of here and tell the insurance company that you were in an accident, hitched a ride to the closest town for medical attention, and when you went back to find the bike, it was gone. No one is going to come all the way out here to try to find it."

I chuckled, "I've been thinking something similar. I thought I could just say that the bike went over a cliff." I paused a minute, "But I think your story that I broke some ribs and we went back to retrieve the bike and couldn't find it is a better lie. You're right. No way in hell the insurance company is going to drive all the way out here to check my story."

In the little two-table restaurant we all ordered a huge breakfast with eggs, ham, coffee from a jar, juice, beans, and toast. Just before it was served, Jake excused himself. "Where ya going?" Tom asked.

"I haven't taken a shit for two or three days. Gotta do it now!"

"Your eggs are going to get cold."

"It'll be messy if I stay!" and he hurried across the street. His eggs were indeed cold by the time he returned ten minutes later. He walked the swagger of a no longer constipated man.

"The whites of your eyes aren't brown any more," Tom joked.

"Yeah," I added, "you're not as full of shit as you were."

"Dave," Jake returned to the unfinished plan, "if you tell that story to the insurance company, we all have to tell them the same story. Let's create a version that we all can agree to and stick to it no matter what."

We batted the story around and soon agreed. The story would stand; I dropped my motorcycle, injured my ribs, and hitched a ride to Morelos. When we went back to get the bike, we couldn't find it and assumed that someone in that drug-infested land had found it and hauled it away.

"You guys are willing to lie for me?"

They both nodded their heads. "That's what friends do."

Jake's streetwise semi-legal experience kicked in, "We can't have any pictures of your bike in the truck. I'll delete everything I have. Do you have any pictures, Tom?"

"Nope, all I have are pictures of earlier in the day."

I'm not sure where the fear of being caught in a lie ends and a true sense of moral integrity begins, but I was aware of the moral crisis for myself. I've always suspected that my morality is more tied to fear of being caught than to personal integrity. At least for me, how others see me governs my behavior more than my "moral character." I don't know how it is for others, but I wonder how often we protect our virtuous persona. Is there really an objective morality outside of cultural rules? It's not that I'd never lied before, everybody I'd ever met lies, cheats, and steals, but I'd rarely drawn others into my deceptions. I am much more comfortable lying in secret. Most of the shadowy things we do or think are done in private because being seen by others in our indiscretion is the most difficult thing to handle.

I sat with my eyes unfocused on the present and stared into the future story I'd created to see what was there, trying to evaluate it. How could I live with it? Could I justify it? After all, I'd paid my insurance premiums for years; I am entitled to accept a payment because I've never made a claim before. How would they ever find out? The insurance industry really owed me money, right? They wouldn't send an adjuster all the way to Morelos, would they?

The thought of abandoning my bike was very difficult and

I wasn't committed yet to leaving so I turned to Jake and Tom and acknowledged, "I will try to find a way out with my bike, but if I can't, then I will count on you to keep our story intact."

Over our dirty plates, cold coffee, and half-eaten toast we solemnly bumped fists to seal our solidarity. Our fabricated story set Jake and Tom free and they no longer carried any responsibility to hang around with me. The story bought their freedom. Within minutes, unfettered, as if their leg irons had been unlocked, they walked across the street and began to pack their bikes for the grueling day ahead.

The lie gave me a roadmap for the way out. I'd abandon my integrity and my bike if necessary and learn to live with my duplicity, but at least I had a chance of getting out alive. All I had to do now was find some sort of transport that would carry both my bike and me on the long journey to safety.

••

The Price of Salvation

It is the map you don't see that causes all the problems.

—Ken Wilbur

The fat woman in the red top also owned a small store that sold sugary cola drinks, peanuts, and chips. After breakfast I walked in, looked at the dusty merchandise on the shelves, and explained to her and her three friends that I needed to find a way back to Guadalajara. With sign language and a few Spanish words, I struggled to ask them if there was a towing company I could hire to haul my bike and me back to civilization.

All speaking at once and very fast, they offered me suggestions and through the commotion I picked out a word I recognized, *autobús*. My eyes widened, "*¿Autobús que viene aquí?*" "A bus comes here?"

"*Sí, Señor. Autobús a Guachochi.*"

I'd already learned from a young man on the street that Guachochi was the closest real town. I finally found Guachochi on my map.

My eyes flitted back and forth among all the women there. "A bus, here? What time does it leave?"

"*Quatro y media.*"

I couldn't understand why it would leave at 4:30 p.m., thinking that it would not drive all night. Besides, how could a bus traverse these roads? I doubted them because no bus I'd ever seen would be able to negotiate the hairpin turns. I kept questioning them, trying to understand the time and reality of an *autobús* and to figure out where to pick it up. Hand gestures and my minimal Spanish left me wondering if I was delusional or understood what I thought I was hearing. I had visions of an air-conditioned 42-foot air-ride Greyhound bus. I could handle that.

Then out of the blue, I caught a word that one of the women used, *avión*, while she made the gesture of a bird flying. Though I'd seen many buzzards circling, I couldn't understand why she was pointing out the birds, but then I heard, "*Señor, Guachochi por avión.*"

I flapped my arms, mimicking the flight of a bird, but they shook their heads, insisted, extended their arms and made the movement of fixed-wing aircraft and repeated, "*¡Señor, Guachochi por avión!*"

"An airplane here? Really? An airplane flies to Guachochi? When?"

"*Hoy por la mañana aquí.*" "Today, in the morning, here" and she pointed up into the hills surrounding the town. I ferreted out the word *limpia* and recognized it as a word our house cleaner uses to talk about cleaning, and I finally understood that the airplane would arrive as soon as the clouds were cleaned from the sky.

Astonished, I couldn't believe it. They were telling me that an airplane flew in and out of Morelos and the ticket office was down the street. They called a ten-year-old boy off the street, spoke some Spanish to him and he grabbed my hand and told me to follow him. A block away he introduced me to his mother and father who ran another store full of Coca Cola, chips, some dusty clothes, and other staples.

"Is there a plane that flies to Guachochi?"

"*Sí, Señor.*"

"How much does it cost?"

"$650 pesos" (about $48.00 USD).

"When does it come?"

"As soon as the clouds clear."

"Today?"

"*¡Sí, Señor, en una hora, más o menos!*"

An airplane could fly me out of here within the hour! I then understood that once a week a small plane flew from Guachochi to this tiny village. In one hour I could be on an airplane to an airport and from there I could hop a flight to Guadalajara and home and safety and a comfortable bed. Every scenario of bumping my way out in a truck, finding a way to get my motorcycle to a dealership to get it fixed, waiting in another strange Mexican city for who knew how long before it would be ready, and then riding it all the way south to Ajijic, vanished in an instant. Oh, please, let there be a seat available.

"Do you want a ticket?"

Without further consideration of consequences or any idea of what I could do with my bike, what to say to the man with the greasy hands, or what to do with the rest of the gear on my bike, I said yes! They gave me a pink slip of paper with number six stamped on it. I got the last seat on a weekly flight out and I had a brand new plan that seemed like salvation. No more struggle, no more suffering, no more worry, and my fear dropped away.

I had less than an hour to finish details, pack my gear, get back to the ticket office, find a ride to the airstrip, and most importantly, try to get on the only telephone in Morelos to call my wife. I hobbled up the street as fast as my frozen legs and recoiling rib allowed. Jake and Tom had spread out their wet camping tarps to dry and were in the final stages of loading their bikes.

"Guys. You'll never guess what happened! I just bought a flight to Guachochi! It leaves in less than an hour. I'm gettin' outta here! Wahoo!"

"You're shitting me." The jealous edge in Tom's voice stung like a scorpion because I knew he was at the end of his energy as well. My premonitions of his tumbling over a cliff returned and I wished he could find permission to end his journey.

"It's the best $50.00 I'll ever spend. Are you still cool about what we're going to tell the insurance company?"

"Yep." They both answered in unison and turned back to their packing.

We gave each other a parting hug. "Keep it up, you guys. I

don't envy your ride. Rubber side down, OK!" I blinked back the tears.

"We'll be alright, take care of yourself, too."

I rushed into the hotel room, hurriedly collected my gear as compactly as I could, and carried it to the street. It was perhaps the biggest error I'd made on this trip.

••

Beauty That Steals the Mind

*I didn't know what to say, my mouth could not speak, my eyes could not
see and something ignited in my soul, fever or unremembered wings and I
went my own way, deciphering that burning fire.*

—Pablo Neruda

In your light I learn how to love.
In your beauty, how to make poems.
You dance inside my chest where no one sees you,
but sometimes I do,
and that sight becomes this art.

—Rumi

I was tired of being lost. I was tired of being scared. I was
tired of being in pain. I was tired of imagining a drug lord's
henchman grabbing me and taking me somewhere from
which I'd never return. I was alone again without the help and
camaraderie of Jake and Tom. All of this made me hurry. Rather than slowing down to sink into wisdom, my focus became
constricted, insensitive, and narrow, as if speed would save me
from whatever was chasing me. In too much of a hurry to keep
my options open, I immediately began to count on the flight
out to be the solution to all that troubled me. The possibility of
escape excited me and suddenly flying out became urgent and
demanded that I make that flight at all costs.

Alongside that insistence even more anxiety inundated me.
Time is running out! What would I do if I missed that flight?
What if the plane couldn't land because of the clouds or if there
were a waiting list and I got bumped off? Would I ever find
another way out? My uncertainty appeared to me as danger.
The thought of waiting for a week in Morelos before the plane
made its weekly return filled me with horror. Suddenly my salvation became the source of even more despair.

Time was rapidly evaporating and it became my new com-
batant, something to be saved, something to be afraid of, and

something that I had to use and conserve or else it would abandon me here. Maybe I'd never get out. The fearful scenario took over my whole being, distorted my sense of time, and created even more dread. I lost touch with my precious and hard-won knowledge that the soul shows its face and make its entrance into the world only when time slows down.

I found myself experiencing the backside of the truth I read on a bumper sticker, "I feel so much better now that I've given up hope." Hope is the fantasy of leaving what is *here* and going to the imagined what is *there*. I couldn't quiet my mind. Looking back, there was no good reason for my urgency to leave Morelos. I was unsure but not in danger. If only I'd taken the day to rest, heal some, orient myself to the village, talk to the people, play with the kids, and call Gloria, I would have recognized that I was not in my full mind and then the remainder of this story might have been simple...or so I imagine now.

Somewhere along life's journey I made a commitment that in all things important, I would make the time to listen to the wisdom of the soul, to wait in quietness until the doors of the soul's perception opened and offered its solution. I've striven to become as aware as others have striven to win. Jake was driven to conquer. I am compelled to know the reality of my soul's insistences, to be honest with myself, and to take ownership for what I do in life. I am obliged to an inner ethic to step out of my stories and live close to the actual data of the world, but I blew it and even as I prepared to leave, a haunting voice told me I was failing. I'd lost myself to the rushing river of fear.

In motorcycle safety we teach not to ride when impaired, when mental and physical functioning is reduced because of stress, tiredness, or dehydration. But how do we recognize, when in the middle of a crisis, that we are morally compromised or impaired by the illusion of time, or reenacting the losses or terrors of childhood? When tired, hungry, stressed or dehydrated, our pattern of behavior regresses and reptilian flight or fight reactions take over. In that state of panic, harmful, dangerous, and even inhuman behaviors seem to make sense. Slowing down is the antidote, but for me at that point, instinct and molasses-slow soul-speed were far apart.

I didn't have much time to call Gloria before the plane left. The public phone at the only booth in town had lost its battle against a raging drunk who smashed it with a rock years ago. As I stood there with a broken receiver in my hand, José, the young son of the ticket seller, who had become my guardian, corralled me and pulled me inside the store to the only telephone in Morelos.

This radiophone operated for only a few hours a day, Monday through Friday. *"Un momentito,"* his mother said with thumb and forefinger very close together when I asked her if I could make a call.

I tried to call as soon as a channel opened up. Several other people came into the store and lined up behind me, breathing down my neck, impatient to call out before the brief calling window closed.

"Now it's ready," she said and handed me the phone. I dialed our number. "Damn!" I didn't hear any of the electronic noise indicating the call had gone through. I tried again and added 045, the prefix used in Mexico when calling outside of the phone zone. This time I heard the dreaded computerized instructions of a rapidly speaking operator in Spanish. I had no idea what she said. All I could do was hand the phone to the clerk. I grimaced with exasperation and shrugged my shoulders to look as forlorn as possible, *"¿Qué pasa, Señora?"*

She took the phone, listened for a moment, and then wrote some numbers on a piece of paper, apparently the number code to activate the radiotelephone. I tried all of those. This time, nothing. I tried again. Again the beloved mechanical voice on the line gave me instructions. I got pissed because I lost the dial tone. I handed the phone back to the *señora*, wrote down my telephone numbers, and signed to her asking if she would dial for me.

Finally she opened her eyes wide, smiled, and offered me the receiver as soon as the phone began to ring at my house. Nothing. No answer. Either Gloria was off on her morning walk or the phone at home wasn't working. I stood with the receiver in my white-knuckled hand, tapping it against the tile counter, my eyes closed, grinding my teeth, and wondered if I should try one more time or give up my place in line. The villagers were silently boring their annoyed stares through my back.

Just then, José broke through my dazed quandary when he rushed into the store, grabbed me by the shirt, pulled me outside and pointed to the sky, *"Señor, Señor, avión aquí!"* Just as he'd indicated, my twin-engine salvation was emerging through the clouds and circling the village.

"Hurry, hurry! We must leave now!"

The man who had sold me the ticket fired up his rig, rushed up the street and threw my stuff into the back of his Jeep Cherokee. He handled my gear with the same lack of precision he used when he welded the doors shut with a couple pieces of second-hand angle iron. The rusting green Jeep had been rolled several times. The jagged heat-blued metal posts from the crudely removed top jutted off the body like stumps in a forest clear cut. The springs of the seats poked through the rotted upholstery so he used several flattened cardboard boxes to save his passengers from being impaled. I winced when he boosted me over the ragged edges of the doors and I sat down on soggy cardboard. With all four tires shooting up rooster tails of dirt behind us, we sped off in his customized-by-crash 4-wheel drive SUV convertible.

His frenzy to get to the airstrip was so intense that I didn't have time to stop by my motorcycle to retrieve more stuff or tell the mechanic what had happened and make some plans with him. With a whoop and a holler, the driver blasted his custom-by-crash Cherokee across ravines and ran over boulders, driving with no regard for the suspension, the tires, or for my agony. Without functioning shock absorbers it bobbed like a boat in a choppy sea. As if he were a starved madman rampaging for his last meal, he blew by other trucks, honking his horn, waving his arms like a rodeo cowboy. Everyone smiled and waved as he drove past.

I swallowed a lot, clamped down hard on my teeth, and choked back my tears as we left town. I'd abandoned my beloved motorcycle, my precious Suzi. I'd given up on her! I'd rationalized my decision to leave her by telling myself I'd never ride again. I kept trying different mental tricks to quell my sadness. *It's only a thing. I can always buy another one. It's my life that matters, not things.* But none of those rationalizations helped fill the guilty emptiness inside. I'd abandoned something I loved. I'd left a bike worth a lot of money. Money and material things still mattered. Pretending otherwise didn't help.

Preoccupations about my motorcycle faded quickly while I held onto the Jeep so I wouldn't get tossed out. Every time the Jeep bounced on a rut or rock, shards of pain spread from my rib through my body as the driver spun this demolished wreck up the hill to the airstrip. What met us there at the gate sent chills through me. Two Federal Police 4 x 4 pickups loaded with five or six officers and a black German shepherd stopped us at the barbed wire entrance to the dirt airstrip.

My assumption that Morelos was too remote to be policed was obviously incorrect. It was crawling with police. The number of police and their intensity when they examined my luggage suggested that this territory was indeed dangerous and must be filled with drug traffickers. It would take only one phone call to the police for the insurance company to see if they could find my bike. While they were scrutinizing my luggage, I heard the familiar sound of Jake and Tom's cycles laboring up the road not far away but there was no way for me to chase them down in order to alter the idiotic deception we'd conjured an hour ago. Fearing that our plan would not work, I couldn't think fast enough to fabricate an alternate story.

The pilot distributed my gear in the rear and I gingerly wormed my way into the back of the six-passenger plane. While I waited for the pilot to get in I thought how ironic it was to be sitting in the cramped seat of a modern Cessna waiting to taxi down the airstrip and be lifted to safety. After struggling for days on the road, I would be out of the Canyon in an hour and a half! I felt like an alien rushed by circumstances from one state of confusion to another. I only knew I was headed out but didn't know where I was going.

As I relaxed in the cabin of that small Cessna I began to recognize the mistakes that had risen from my rushed escape plan. Wanting to save my life even if it made me lie and cheat the insurance company, I hadn't taken the time to walk down to the river, let it speak its wisdom to me, and pick up a souvenir stone. Instead, I jumped for the only rope I could see in that survival-bound state. After the fear subsided a bit I saw just how little separated a mature resolution to my situation and a panicked retreat. For want of a day's rest, proper nutrition, and long drinks of water, I'd lost contact with the part of my mind that would have told me to wait until my fear diminished enough so I could access inner resources.

In order to climb out of the deep Canyon, the plane spiraled up in a tight left-hand bank that gave me a clear view of the terrain below. I kept trying to locate Jake and Tom as the plane coiled into the sky. With each ring of elevation, I exhaled with relief even as I shuddered. All the way to the horizon, I saw nothing but ridges, ravines, cliffs, trees, peaks, and the copper-colored road that serpentined up and down and into their future. I was very glad to be here and not there. I worried for Jake and Tom's safety.

The higher the airplane climbed, the more enthralled I became with the vastness and beauty of *Barrancas del Cobre*. The plane flew from Morelos up one of the six river systems that feed into Rio Fuerte. Whereas the Grand Canyon is desert with virtually no vegetation, the chasms I was flying over were thickly wooded. All I could see from the air were green-carpeted walls, granite outcroppings, mountain peaks, and valleys. Then it finally made sense why there were no tourist signs that pointed to THE *Barrancas del Cobre*. It was too vast! My heart was broken open by the beauty I witnessed and my breathing quickened with amazement.

As the plane rose through the evaporating clouds that hovered in the morning air, my own islands of clarity began to emerge like the tops of mountains poking through fog. My heart flew open at the stunning panorama before me. Waves of wonder flooded over me. My eyes, my breath, and especially my heart reeled and I experienced a mystical intimacy with everything in the world. Love in its purest form spellbound me. Rumi's words: "In your light I learn how to love..." made sense.

This ecstasy dissolved my sense of time and I suddenly found myself *knowing* something about my father. This was the same wonder that burst into him when he first encountered the Rocky Mountains in Montana. He must have been taken by the astounding panorama the mountains offered him. I realized then that his devotion to splendor often got lost behind his strident Baptist theology. It was Beauty he worshiped, not Jesus! The tone in his voice when he spoke of nature was reverent; the tone in his voice when he preached was rehearsed. While looking out of the airplane I experienced what he lived for and what he lived from.

He had transferred this love of Beauty to me, and if my life's work was connected to my father, it came from the unspoken truth that bound us: the soul is born in Beauty, feeds on Beauty, and requires Beauty for its sustenance. How many of our pioneering fathers had been stunned by this Beauty, but like me had gotten so caught up in trying to get somewhere else that they never allowed themselves to be fully here? How many of them, at the behest of nature, experiencing similar dissolving movements in the soul, lacked the skill to express in words how their hearts melted? How many, in reverence, were hushed into silence by an explosion of raw Beauty and fled from its potency because entanglements with the sensuality of nature demand a softness and vulnerability that our culture discourages? An apt line from Emily Dickinson came to mind, "The truth dazzles gradually, or else the world would be blind." Beauty dazzles so completely that we are often left speechless.

Places with this kind of power posses us, compel us to go there and experience something alive, new, and humbling. They act as a Siren-call to the soul to "come visit me." They invite us to give up our ideas of control and submit to the unspeakable. The power of the Canyon's call took hold and dragged me not only to the Canyon but also to this mystical moment in which nothing but love and connection to all things reigned.

The drive to find oneself in such mystical experiences of beauty is at the core of every human being. Homer said, "In it is love, and in it desire, and in it blandishing persuasion that steals the mind even from the wise." Every man I've ever had a heart to heart talk with knows this place in his being that longs to heed the call and yield, if only for a moment, to that mind-stealing seduction, even though it may lead to destruction. The soul requires moments when it loses itself to the power of Beauty.

I was grasped by what I couldn't grasp. I realized that the draw to this area blinded me from making rational decisions. Just like every man who is driven by his desire to watch a beautiful woman lift her skirt to reveal the glory waiting there, I watched, riveted, as the clouds dissipated, disrobing the Canyon's grandeur.

Every time the Sirens call, it seems worthwhile... at least for a moment.

..

Judge the Moth by the Beauty of the Candle

Many men go fishing all of their lives without knowing that it is not fish they are after.

—Henry David Thoreau

Even while I swooned inside my mystical union with the Canyon, I also began to mourn the loss of my bike. The decision to leave it began a tangible ache in the center of my chest for I knew that I'd never return to that area again. My new relationship to the Canyon also brought Tom and Jake into focus. I didn't like that I'd drawn Jake and Tom into an agreement to defraud. The more I thought about it, the tighter the knot squeezed. I was on my way out but I was still stuck.

If it was this easy to get out, why didn't you stay a while longer to take better care of things? my relentless inner accuser sneered.

Because I have a broken rib, I don't know the language, I'm all alone, I can barely move, I'm too exhausted, and there's no turning back. Leave me alone! It amazed me how quickly that old voice of shame came to nail me. I reflected on the talk Tom and I had shared in Mazatlán when I explained to him the role of shame that makes a bad situation worse.

The roar of the engine couldn't drown out my inner turmoil, nor could the stunning beauty below me. I watched the altimeter as the plane climbed to 9,000 feet. Because the three of us had approached from sea level, we never arrived at any of the spectacular vistas, but now in the airplane I experienced unparalleled grandeur. I was thrilled by the awe-inspiring vertical cliffs, serpentine rivers flowing like brown worms through a maze of green V-shaped ridges and valleys, and the towering spires of countless mountain peaks as far north and south as I could see.

The plane lifted past the last lip of the gorge and the scenery changed as suddenly as if someone had turned an album page.

The shock of flat, vibrant green farmland literally took my breath away. I imagined that on a clear day one could stand on the edge of the cliff and see all the way to the ocean 200 miles away. Ahead of us lay farmland, houses, fences, and straight roads, and above all, asphalt, blessed blacktop. What relief just to see civilization again!

When the plane taxied to a stop in Guachochi, a 12,000-person town a few miles from the rim, we were met by four heavily armed *Federales*. I was brought up short by their immediate appearance at the plane, their stern no nonsense stance, hands on their automatic weapons, and the way they scrutinized us. Two boarded the plane to search for drugs and two others ushered me to the security gate. Drug war fever hung like a shroud at the airport. I didn't know if this inspection was normal or if I'd landed in the middle of Mexico's underbelly of crime. Several of my friends who had lived for many years in Mexico had warned me about the dangers of being robbed, but in my naivety I'd dismissed them all. I was not quite so cavalier at this point. The number of police I'd seen in just a few hours made me feel fortunate that we hadn't run into more trouble, but it also diminished my self-condemnation for being as afraid as I was. We'd been swimming in dangerous waters.

I didn't have time to organize my gear in Morelos before flying out, so wrestling my loose collection of motorcycle luggage from the belly of the plane presented its own set of problems. I had three primary pieces of luggage: a magnetized tank bag that doubled as a backpack, a heavy-duty nylon bag, and an expensive 60-liter fiberglass "top case." To the bag I'd bungeed my tent and zipped my heavy fluorescent riding jacket over that. To haul this load around I found it most comfortable to hold my left arm hard against my ribcage to immobilize the left side of my body. Staggering with my load, I looked like a man headed for a refugee camp. Maybe my filthy clothes or the way I dragged my gear or the glaze that had fallen over my eyes softened the scrutiny of the police, and they gave only superficial attention to my gear and waved me through. I didn't have language to let anyone know that I wanted help. I threaded my gear through the turnstile and stumbled into the street not knowing what to do next.

An assertive taxi driver greeted me in Spanish first and then in relatively good English, "Do you need a ride?"

"Yes."

"Where are you going?"

"I need to get to Guadalajara. Where is the closest airport that will fly me there?"

"There's an airport in Hidalgo del Parral. A bus leaves in a half hour."

"Can we get there in time?"

"Yes, the bus station is only ten minutes away."

Maybe by evening I could be home safe and comfortable if we hurried! My pulse rate jumped at this possibility. On the way to the bus station I turned my attention towards Gloria in Ajijic. My cell phone had run out of minutes so I asked the taxi driver if there was a place in town to buy a new chip that would work in the state of Chihuahua. I knew I was pushing the time envelope again but at that point my focus had turned to home and I wanted more than anything to make contact with her.

"Do I have enough time to buy a chip and a ticket before the bus leaves?"

He called the bus station and reassured me that I would have time. They took forever to install and verify a new chip. Each minute increased my anxiety about catching the bus. The driver was waiting for me when I finally got out of the store. Just down the street he dropped me off in the middle of a crowd of indigenous locals waiting for the bus. The men wore stiff white cowboy hats and clean starched white shirts. Many of the women wore brilliant yellow and vibrant blue pleated skirts with embroidered white blouses that set off their leathered and burnished skin. I was struck by the sheen of their raven hair that was pulled back from their faces by colorful beads. The children were all scrubbed, students wore modern backpacks, and everyone hung around on the sidewalk, sitting on suitcases and boxes or balanced on their haunches against the wall. The beauty and calm of these travelers was something I'd never witnessed before, as if the beauty of the Canyon had inspired them to display their own splendor. These were the famed Tarahumara. I'd been warned about the "chicken buses" and imagined that I might have to share my seat with a pig, but that anxiety vanished as soon as I walked into that crowd. I didn't see any livestock

I wonder who was more impacted, them or me. It must have been quite a sight for them to observe this wide-eyed, wounded gringo, grimacing in pain, struggling with filthy mud-caked florescent motorcycle gear, walk into the ticket office. No one offered to help me horse all this gear through the narrow ticket office door. I felt as self-conscious as if I were on stage with all eyes on me.

To my complete relief, the lady at the ticket desk had an available ticket. No seat assignment, just a slip of paper with a blue stamp showing the date. I didn't know it then, but they oversell seats all the time, and as I would learn later, some passengers would stand in the aisle for the three-hour trip to Parral.

On the second day of our trip, Montezuma had begun his revenge. Fortunately he kept his mischief focused on the lower end of my digestive tract. Periodically my ass lost its discernment and, misinterpreting a fart, left a stinging brown streak in my shorts. My bowels never hardened up the entire trip, and as soon as I saw the bathroom sign, all parts of me rushed toward the door screaming for relief. I was sure the overused bathroom in the dingy bus ticket office would be urine soaked as so many are. I didn't want to put my gear down on the floor, but wondered if it would be safe to leave it unsecured on the bench. On the vacant seat next to the one I was about to smother with my stuff, a thick-waisted woman wearing the typical embroidered skirt, white blouse and multicolored scarf looked up at this filthy man moving into the chair beside her.

How do they keep their whites so white and the colors so vibrant? I wondered if she'd steal my gear or protect it.

She smiled at me with the shy graciousness so characteristic of the Tarahumara and I knew my gear would be safe while I did my business.

Unfortunately, I discovered that the combination of Montezuma's visitations and the pounding my butt had taken from the bike caused me to develop a hemorrhoid the size of an overgrown grape. Its size concerned me, but any pain hadn't yet wormed its way into consciousness to let me know that my ass needed attention. However, feeling the sting as I voided on the first actual toilet in a long time, I got a very clear message to take care of this precious part in need of repair. Like a child who trips and falls will look around to find his mother before he begins to wail, my tail waited until now to announce its displeasure.

I didn't need another thing to stress me, so I tried to relieve some of the suffering by reminding my ass of an experience earlier in my life. It seemed a bit strange to carry on a conversation with my ass, but it was crying out so I thought it deserved some looking after. I told it of the great secret taught to me by a dead rabbit.

Fifteen years ago I'd driven from Portland to my lake cabin to do what I loved the most: sit on my deck, get quiet in the serenity of that reflective lake, and write poetry. I plunked myself on my favorite chair and instantly a rancid smell shattered my calm. I looked into the breeze and saw the rotting carcass of a large rabbit on my neighbor's dock. Its noxious fumes wafted directly across the lawn and straight into my waiting nostrils. I began fussing whether I should just move to another place or dig a hole to bury the rabbit. If I buried it, would it contaminate my shovel and would the shovel then carry some sort of virus? How could I decontaminate my shovel? If I got closer, would its stink leap on me like a skunk's spray? Why did it die? If I pushed it into the water, would it pollute the lake and poison the fish? These thoughts distracted me from my usual intimacy with the lake. I got more and more pissed off, trying to figure out what to do.

Just then a new thought came, "I don't think I have ever let myself actually experience the smell of putrid. It's the fear of sitting all day in the putrid smell that is causing all my suffering! So why not take this opportunity to truly experience putrid? It's not going to kill me."

I put down my pen and paper, inhaled long and deeply through my nose, and experienced the acrid stinging in my nostrils. Almost instantly that bite went away and all discomfort disappeared. Then I understood a principle that has helped guide my life and is one of the very few things I really know: when I bring my attention to the physical experience of the moment, the pain and the suffering dramatically lessen. Normally we do everything we can to make the pain go away, which causes the body to constrict and lock in the hurt. However, if we open ourselves to our actual sensations, relax, breathe, and give the feelings room, they diminish quickly. Suffering is debilitating, not the pain itself. It's the *idea* that something will be awful that makes it awful, not the experience itself. It's just like riding in the mud. Dive into it and it goes away.

With that graphic reminder, I took a deep breath and turned my attention to the searing fire from the protrusion. Almost immediately the pain left. I hauled myself off the toilet seat and anxiously stepped back into the bus station's lobby to discover that my gear was untouched. There was quite a commotion when I walked from the shadows of the ticket office into the sunlight. Everyone looked at me and I heard someone shout as a ferocious looking Mexican man charged up to me, looked me square in the eye, and quite aggressively challenged me. I didn't understand him but finally recognized his demand for *seiscientos cinquenta pesos* ($650 pesos). I'd forgotten to pay the pilot for the flight out! With groveling and sincere apologies, I paid him his due.

Just then the bus pulled out of its garage to load passengers and what seemed like a thousand Mexicans rushed for the front door to get a seat. I had to worm my way through the line-up to get my luggage into the cargo bay of the bus. I was determined to find a seat. The battle for a seat was not a shoving match like I'd experienced at a soccer game, and I grabbed a window seat near the front of the bus and tenderly lowered my complaining body into it.

The bus was a fairly modern Greyhound type, not one of the infamous "chicken buses." I'd managed to buy some water before we pulled away. *Everyone ought to have this kind of experience*, I thought to myself as I marveled at the indigenous people boarding the bus. Tarahumara women with multicolored shawls, spectacular dresses, scarves wrapped around weathered faces, mothers with babies swaddled in woven blankets, teenagers with cell phones stuck in their ears, toothless men, pure white hats, pressed white shirts, all staring at this dirty white guy having a hard time breathing. The aisles filled with standing people. I was not going to show any chivalry and offer my seat to anybody.

The bus sea-sawed its way into the narrow street and as soon as it got underway and I settled in, I punched in the numbers and called Gloria. She hadn't heard from me for several days and she knew that while I was in the Canyon I'd be out of cell phone range. As usual, her voice was excited and friendly, relieved that I'd made it. Really happy to hear me, she eagerly asked, "How are you my love?"

I choked up and for a few moments couldn't utter a word. I finally managed to speak through my sobs and squeeze out, "I'm alive. I wrecked my bike. I have a broken rib."

She couldn't make sense out of what I was saying. "Where are you?"

I tried in vain to gather myself to speak. It must have been awful for her in those few minutes as I wrestled for composure that wouldn't come no matter how hard I tried. I finally pulled myself together, "We were on the road from hell. We never should have been there. I left my bike in the Canyon. I don't care if I ever ride again!"

"Where are you? What happened? Are you OK? Are you in the hospital? Oh dear!"

Her questions flooded and more of the emotion I couldn't afford in the Canyon burst like a geyser. I tried again to explain, "I dropped my bike and broke a rib. I'm in great pain. I had to leave the bike in the Canyon and I don't think I'll ever ride again."

"Oh, David!" I could feel the deep sympathy and concern in her voice. "I don't care about the bike, it's only money, you're alive, and that's all that matters!"

Her tone begged for more.

"I lost my bike. Jake and Tom are on the absolute road from hell and I am scared to death for them. We never should have been on these roads and I don't know if they will make it out!" I choked up and the tears just rolled down my cheeks while I struggled to find an island of control again.

"Where are you?" Her gentle voice made me wish that I could simply be transported into her arms.

"On a bus just leaving Guachochi headed for Parral." I was quite unable in that state of mind to help clarify for her where in the world I was.

I explained my situation as succinctly as I could and before I could explore any options, I heard the cell phone gurgle and spit, and I knew my $200-peso chip was heaving its last gasps before it expired.

"Gloria, my minutes are running out. I am on a bus and will be out of range for three hours. I will call you when I get to the airport at Parral!"

I hated to leave her hanging like that. I imagined what it was like for her to be cut off from her sobbing, pained, broken husband somewhere in Mexico on a bus headed for an unknown city. Inflicting this anxiety on her caused me as much suffering as the other physical tortures I'd been through.

The depth of the connection we'd established in the years of our relationship is unspoken most of the time but serves as bedrock for both of us. When I heard her invitation for me to open everything I'd experienced, it unzipped the armor of the necessary toughness I'd wrapped around myself. All I wanted at that point was to be free to release the wide complexity of my feelings--the anger at having to leave, shame for falling so deeply into despair, remorse that I'd lost my integrity, troubled that I'd been so passive and not demanded that we turn around, proud that I'd gone as far as I had, amazed at what I'd learned, stunned by the beauty of the Canyon, broadened by having met some of the indigenous people, and the morbid fear I was suffering thinking about the rest of the ride for Tom and Jake. Within the safety of Gloria's wide and loving arms and our unconditional commitment to each other, I could be everything I was and without fear of recrimination.

After she had demonstrated her love for me in this way, I began to find important parts of myself in my weakness and vulnerability. During my three-hour bus trip to Parral I didn't locate my center by any tough-minded macho pride; I found myself by allowing my desperation and the wide array of my emotions to be real. The putrid rabbit had taught me to get real and personal with whatever the moment brings. The way Gloria and I worked in our forty-year relationship created a safe place where we could share our deepest secrets, the dirt of our personalities, our actual hopes and doubts, our vulnerabilities, our inflated and diminished views of ourselves.

Despite our differences, we had bounced and tumbled in the slurry of our lives together, rounding and polishing each other to create the capacity to be authentically naked with each other. We had worked through times of bliss and times of thinly veiled dislike to arrive at a place in our relationship that was a safe haven for both of us. I didn't keep myself from weeping as I traveled in the bus, feeling her deep support, and I dropped away from any need for pretense. Finding strength in my weakness, I looked forward to our next conversation when I could tell her more of the story and let her see and feel the trauma I'd just been through.

Meanwhile, while I was on my motorcycle trip, she had discovered that an infestation of termites had tunneled through the concrete floor of our house and feasted on the doorframes. They had set their sights on our expensive wooden cabinets. She hired a termite eradication company to come in and nuke the subterranean infestation. That meant that when I called, three men were busy in the house hammer-drilling 200 half-inch holes through the floor tiles to eliminate the threat of the termites ever coming back again. The house was a cacophony of hammer drills, singing Mexicans, and blaring stereos.

They were in the house when I called and Gloria turned to them in desperate hope that they could help her figure out where I was. She pulled out maps of Mexico and tried to give them her English version of a Mexican town she couldn't spell or pronounce. They couldn't locate where I was but these gracious men provided a sort of support system for her, offering to translate if another call came. Gloria instructed them that if she came out with a phone at her ear and waving at them, they were to stop immediately and come to the phone to help her. I didn't know it then but they'd already offered to drive anywhere in Mexico to pick up my bike and me.

I'd purposely hidden the small detail that I was planning to put one over on the insurance company to spare her the agony of living with a lie. I was trapped by my hastily concocted plan to cheat the insurance company. What seemed like salvation just a few hours ago now seemed like a very bad idea. I stared through my sad reflection in the window, wondering if I would ever find myself again. I'd hidden significant information from Gloria and didn't know how to come clean.

••

The Real Way Out

A partner is not there to help you get you where you want to go, but a person to be with you where you are.

—Anonymous

Now, sitting back in the bus, heading for what I thought was an airport and the possibility of home, a good bed, and Gloria's comfort, I began to relax into life again. Memories of the roads in the Canyon kept flashing in my mind. They now seemed like labyrinthine river tributaries and we had been trying to swim upstream to the headwaters to find the Holy Grail. We'd scrambled up roads that quietly reduced to a trickle and petered out in someone's front yard. We tried everything to find the main artery that would lead us to our goal, wondering if this road would bring us closer, trying to read the tracks to find the road most traveled. What started as a journey into Beauty became an ordeal that could have cost our lives.

Butting up against the futility of finding our way cut us off from everything we had ever known. Deprived of familiar comforts and having no road signs, we were quickly forced into a dependency that unified and protected us. The terror of riding down another dead-end road wouldn't leave me. Now, in the relative safety of the bus, I wasn't sure if Tom and Jake had abandoned me or I them. I couldn't shake my remorse for having caused a disruption to their trip. They had become like brothers to me, and even though I now traveled worlds apart from them, part of me still rode with them in their terror.

It was a troubling ride for me for other reasons. The fact that I hadn't told Gloria the whole truth weighed me down more and more. Bearing this secret alone would certainly drive a damaging wedge in our relationship. I came to realize that it was my own condemnation, not hers that I really feared. She'd proven over and over again that I could trust her with the less than noble sides of my personality.

The bus was crammed with a variety of people and as we traveled, the gentle sense of community that often develops with fellow travelers deepened my internal struggle. I began to look at those around me and connected with them. We were all in the hands of the bus driver and had turned our lives over to this temporary pilot. In this spirit of community I realized that the mechanic with the ham bone hands was no longer a stranger but someone's son and someone's father, a man with a name. By leaving my motorcycle in his yard I'd just put him in a terrible situation. It would have been different if I'd left my bike on the edge of the road or pushed it over a cliff, but it now sat out in the open for the whole village to see. This new, powerful, abandoned *moto* and what happened to the gringo who left it there would be the talk of the town!

Before I saw the Federal Police at the landing, I'd assumed that there wouldn't be any "law" this far away from civilization but now I knew differently. If I reported my bike stolen and they were to send the police to find it, then my motorcycle conspicuously sitting in the man's yard would be found out and the innocent mechanic would be charged with theft. He would be accused. What a mess I'd created. My salvation would cost him.

As soon as I imagined that my error could jeopardize his life, I knew that I wouldn't be able to perpetrate the lie. By the time I was halfway to Parral, I made the decision to be completely truthful to the insurance company and let the chips fall where they may. If I lost my bike, so be it. I made a decision to restore my integrity.

My concern for Tom's safety tormented me as well. His dirt dirt-riding skills were as limited as mine. His BMW had taken a real beating on the roads. The bracket to one of his hard saddlebags had broken and bag was now strapped on top of Jake's already loaded down bike, his brakes were funky, and he was running on a tire that we'd sealed by pouring repair goo into it. We didn't know how long it would last before it needed repair again, but most ominously, he was as exhausted as I was. His words to me over breakfast earlier that morning haunted me, "I feel too tired to ride far today. I shouldn't be here on these roads. A wreck could pull my hip apart and I'd be in deep shit."

Having seen the endless switchbacks and red roads winding over many steep mountains they'd have to cross made it worse for me. I was sick thinking about it.

In the relative calm of the underpowered bus, my senses began to return. The open windows let the smell of the recent desert rain soften the unmistakable stench of too many sweaty bodies stuffed into a cramped space on a steamy afternoon. Going up hills, the driver had to drop down into first or second gear but the relaxed pace of the day gave me opportunity to experience the high desert of the state of Chihuahua. Out of the Canyon, roads no longer seemed horrible. I looked to the delicious curves ahead and thought how sweet it would be to ride on these. The statement I'd made to Gloria that I'd never ride again dissolved like sugar in water. Of course I'd ride again. Regret settled over me and I knew that getting out of the Canyon was only the beginning.

Later that afternoon, the bus pulled into the city of Hidalgo del Parral and stopped on the street. Still in shock and in pain, with my eyes wide open to yet another new island of humanity, I unloaded my gear onto a busy sidewalk and immediately had to fend off people offering to help, wanting a handout, or hawking trinkets. *Leave me alone so I can gather myself and decide what to do next.* Then a man emerged from the chaos, gestured to my gear on the dirty sidewalk, "¿Necesita taxi?"

I turned to see an elderly taxi driver and answered in my broken Spanish, "Yes, I need to go to the airport. I need to fly to Guadalajara."

"There isn't an airport here; the closest one is in Chihuahua City."

The groans that escaped me this time were not due to pain, but exasperation. I just wanted to get home! "But in Guachochi they told me I could catch a flight here in Parral."

Shrugging with the universal shoulders to ears, "I'm sorry. They gave you the wrong information. You'll have to take a bus to Chihuahua to get a flight to Guadalajara. There's no airport here."

He must have sensed that I was near collapse. He was kind and spoke enough English that I relaxed again. He drove me to a hotel that was moderately priced, close to the bus station, and checked me in. He waited until I'd registered and then he carried all my bags to the room. Three things now dominated my thinking, buying cell phone minutes, finding a pharmacy to replace the pain meds, and eating a good meal.

I'd left Gloria in a terrible fix when my minutes ran out in Guachochi. I checked into the hotel and asked the receptionist, "Where's the closest place to buy Telcel minutes?

"Next door."

"And where can I buy some pain pills?" She pointed three blocks down the street.

"And where can I get a beer and a good meal."

"Across the street and down two blocks."

I loaded my cell phone with enough minutes this time, walked back to my room, dialed home, and held my breath as the phone rang, "Hello."

"Oh, Gloria, I'm so glad I got you. Sorry I got cut off like we did, but I just bought some minutes and we should be good to talk for a while."

"Sweetie, where are you? At the airport? How are you?" My tears, like an artesian well, rose to my eyes again.

"No, I am in a hotel in Hidalgo del Parral. I just got in. I was given the wrong information in Guachochi. I thought there was an airport here but it turns out the closest airport is in Chihuahua City. I don't have the energy to travel any more. I need to spend the night here."

"I am confused, where in Mexico are you? I tried to find you on the map but couldn't. My love, how are you?"

"I am so sore, so tired, and so afraid for Jake and Tom. I saw the roads they had to travel. Jake is tough, nothing will stop him. I don't think Tom will make it."

"How bad are your broken ribs? It sounds like you're having a hard time breathing. Is anything else wrong?" *Did she know already why I'd been so vague with her?*

"I think I broke only one rib. It's hard to tell because I'm so bruised and sore. It's hard to breathe, and dragging my gear around is a pain in the ass. I just clamp down my teeth and do what I have to do. When we're done, I'll go get some meds. A woman in the Canyon gave me six or eight amazing pills, but they're gone. God, the roads were awful. You won't believe the crap we rode through! Mud and rain and washed-out roads. There wasn't any place to stay, no food. We never should have been on those roads!"

Everything I wanted to say to her all hit my mouth at the same time. I could feel the pressure building to tell her the story, unload it, rage about it, and share it. I tried to get underneath the depth of my horror, to pull it out of my psyche so I could go on.

Impatient to tell me some crucial things before my minutes ran out, she interrupted me, "David, sweetheart, we will have time to talk later, but there are some things you must do as soon as possible."

"Gloria, before you go on, I need to come clean. When we were having breakfast this morning, the three of us decided to concoct a story for the insurance company, telling them my bike had been stolen. I was vague when I called you from Guachochi because I didn't want to force you to lie to the insurance company, but riding in the bus with all the innocent Mexicans, I decided that I wouldn't implicate anyone." And then I fessed up. "I left my bike in a mechanic's yard because I was so desperate to fly out. I gotta be honest."

How good it is to have married an understanding woman. "The most important thing was to get you out of the Canyon.

Don't worry about it; your life is so much more important than the bike. You're out, we'll figure out the rest later." A burden lifted as the breadth of Gloria's empathy reminded me of the deep nest we had become for each other.

Gloria still didn't have a clue as to my whereabouts. "I've spent most of the time since you called talking to the insurance company. We have travel insurance on the motorcycle and they're obligated to retrieve the bike."

"Really?" I didn't know that I had travel assistance or I wouldn't have gone through all this mental torture. I thought we had only theft insurance.

"Yes, you're entitled to two nights in a hotel, all meals, and a rental car and transportation home. Don't worry about the money. Just keep your receipts. Listen! Before you get on the plane to come home, you have to file an insurance claim in the state of Chihuahua! You must do this ASAP. I've been talking to an agent in Monterrey. His name is Sebastian." She gave me the claim number and his telephone number. She repeated, "You must call him right away!"

As soon as we hung up I called Sebastian who was the supervisor for all the insurance claims made by gringos in Mexico. His English was broken but he understood enough and told me that indeed I needed to make my claim right away. "You're in Parral, right?"

"Yes."

"And you want to fly back to Guadalajara. OK, take a bus from Parral and when you get to Chihuahua City, call Ramón. He is the insurance adjuster that handles all the gringo claims in that city. He will come to your hotel and make your claim. Don't worry, *Señor*, we will take care of you and find your motorcycle."

My load began to lift! From the opposite ends of the 700 miles that separated us, Gloria and I went to work on the Internet to book a flight from Chihuahua to Guadalajara. Because I was still a day's bus ride from Chihuahua, I couldn't get back home for another two days. With the plane reservation out of the way, I bought a bus ticket to Chihuahua and walked across the street to eat. I wanted comfort food. I ordered a greasy hamburger and large plate of french-fries.

In the morning the hotel manager had one of his staff help me schlep my gear to the bus station. What a joy for me to be inside a plush Mexican bus. I'd never been on a more comfortable trip. The seats reclined to near horizontal, a movie played on the monitor, and the air-ride suspension had me floating to Chihuahua. As soon as the taxi dropped me off and I checked into the hotel, I called Ramón and we agreed to meet in two hours in the lobby.

I'd hoped that an adjuster in Chihuahua would have command of the English language, however, when we met, I struggled to communicate what had happened, where it happened, and where the bike was. We didn't understand 20% of what each other said.

"What was the name of the mechanic?" Good question, but I had no idea.

"What was his address?"

"There were no street signs in the village. He lived on the edge of town."

"What did he look like?"

"Greasy, large belly, hands like a tree stump, mustache, black hair, olive skin.

I tried to explain where the bike was.

Ramón looked confused, "Where is this *Morelos?*" I brought out my map and showed him a very small dot at the bottom of the Canyon. He gulped. "This Morelos is not the Morelos I know!" He showed me his city Morelos that was only a few miles from Chihuahua, quite a contrast to this speck in the Canyon several hundred miles away. *"¡Ay yi yi!"*

"What happened?" I told him the story exactly as it happened, but because he couldn't understand much of my English, he threw up his hands in exasperation and asked me to write my official story inside a two-inch space on a multi-sheet carbon form. The pen had a thick point and I was quite concerned that whoever had to decipher my scrawled account would have difficulty reading it.

After we wrestled and mangled our English/Spanish conversation, we agreed that he would send in a truck the first thing in the morning, find the bike, and take it to an authorized Suzuki dealer in Chihuahua to repair what had broken when I crashed. He promised that when it was repaired, the dealership would call me to have me drive it back home.

I had a hard time believing that he could send a truck to retrieve it. I repeated in the best way I could, "You will go into the Canyon, pick up the bike from the mechanic's yard, and haul it to the dealership in Chihuahua? Is this correct?"

After we settled other details, I emotionally released the task of retrieving my bike to the insurance company and I walked to the pool. I didn't have a swimming suit with me and no one else was poolside, so I stripped down to my scaly underwear and took a dip. I'd forgotten to leave my motorcycle key, so after dinner I went back to the lobby and arranged with the hotel manager to give the key to Ramón. The manager, who had lived for a long time in the United States, and I hit it off immediately and swapped stories about California and Mexico. I told him the short version of my drama and decided to ask him for a favor, "I don't know anyone here in Chihuahua City, and my motorcycle is supposed to come here for repair. I am not sure if I will need to, but if necessary, could I call you and have the dealership leave my bike in your yard until I heal enough to get back here to ride it home?"

"Of course, *Señor!*" He smiled big, "It would be a privilege for me to help!" He gave me his phone number and the number of his son. I forced 200 pesos into his hand and bid him goodbye.

I swallowed two pain pills just before going to bed and I slept strong and deep, thinking maybe things would turn out all right after all. I was clean. Surely the gods must be smiling on my decision to step back into integrity.

Two weeks later, sleazy Ramón disappeared from the insurance company with the key to my bike, the unfiled insurance report buried in his briefcase, and no forwarding address.

··

You Had to Have Been There

Seeker, there is no path. The path is made by walking.

—Antonio Machado

Gloria's face lit up when she saw me walk down the steps of the airplane. She had the smile of someone relieved to see her loved one return, but sad to see her loved one in pain. She looked beyond the pain in my body, trying to reach me where I really hurt. She hugged me gingerly, careful not to add to my misery. "Which rib?" The way she stroked my arm worked magic. I nearly dissolved again. Into my chest she cried, "Oh, David. I'm so glad to see you! You don't look so good. You've lost a lot of weight."

By now it had been three days since I'd left Morelos. The first thing I asked her, "Gloria, have you heard anything from Jake and Tom? I'm so afraid for them. You couldn't believe the roads."

"Yes, we just heard from Tom earlier this morning. Shortly after you flew out, Tom had a serious wreck, nearly went over the cliff. He turned back and Jake went on ahead and we haven't heard from him."

"Was Tom hurt? Where is he?"

"He's OK but was apparently scared to death. Ironically, he was in Chihuahua just a few blocks from you last night and is on a plane headed for home right now."

"God! Thank goodness." I started to choke up with relief but the conveyor belt saved me from embarrassment when it began to bring the luggage and for the first time in a long time someone was there to help me. "Here, let me get it for you. Do you have anything else?"

Together we carried my gear to the curb. "Stay here, I'll get the car. I had to park on the other side of the terminal. No need to carry your stuff there. It'll take a few minutes. I'll drive."

I settled into the passenger seat and when we'd cleared the congestion of the airport and gotten on the road to Ajijic, we resumed where we'd left off, "What happened to Tom? What did you mean that we were next to each other in Chihuahua? Have you talked to him?"

"I've been talking to Susan. She got a call from Tom's wife Theresa early this morning who told her that shortly after they left you on Monday, Tom piled up his bike. They had a huge fight there on the road, separated, and Tom returned to Morelos to see if he could find a ride out."

"What about his BMW?"

"Apparently he just gave his bike away."

"Gave it away! Are you sure? Damn, I knew they were headed for trouble, I could feel it in my bones. Jake went on without him? Have we heard anything else?"

"Nope."

On the drive back home I would often dissolve, overwhelmed with emotion as I gave her the details of what we'd been through. Back on my terrace overlooking Mt. Garcia, with ice packs stacked around my ribcage and some real food in my belly, I called Susan to get any details she had. "Any news from Jake?"

"No. The last anyone has seen or heard of him was when he stormed off after Tom turned back."

"Are you scared?"

"Oh, yeah, but he is a very strong man and a strong rider! He'll be OK."

"He is an amazing rider, much stronger than Tom or me. What else do you know about Tom? Is he OK?"

"He called his wife late last night and told her that he gave his bike away to the local authorities in exchange for a way out. She's enraged! She told me, and I quote, 'That asshole left his $11,000 bike in the Canyon. He is going to have to sell his Harley here in Canada to pay for that!'"

"That's too bad. I completely understand why he'd do that.

I can't describe how awful it was! Did you say that Tom is in Houston right now? Do you have his telephone number?"

Immediately after we hung up I called him, "Oh, my god, Tom, how good to hear your voice. How the hell are you? What happened? From the air I saw the roads you guys had to travel and I've been scared shitless for you ever since." My eyes filled again as I tried to keep my composure. "I'm so glad you made it!"

"The roads got worse after we left Morelos. They were awful, Dave. I was still tired when we left. We were only two hours out of Morelos and I was headed up a very steep section of road. I hit a big rock in the middle of the road, which threw my bike up to the left. I over-corrected and headed toward a 1,000-foot cliff on my right. The next thing I remember is Jake looking down at me checking to see if I'm OK. My tire was four fucking inches from the cliff. I'm lying on my back 15 feet in front of the downed bike. I mean, four inches from that cliff. I must have flipped over the handlebars and knocked myself out. I'm lucky to be alive!"

"Man, I saw this scene in my mind. So then what? Susan said that you and Jake had a huge fight."

"No shit. I sat on a rock for a while and after I pulled myself together I told him, 'I'm not riding any further. I can't go on. I'm going back to Morelos!' We sat down on the red dirt, overlooking the cliff, and I asked him for a drink of water. My water bottle must have fallen off. He didn't want to give me a drink but finally threw the bottle at me and said, 'Take care of your own shit!'

"He stormed over to my bike, picked it up like it was a piece of paper, and got it on its kickstand. I finally rearranged my gear and turned my bike back down the hill toward Morelos. Jake wouldn't haul my broken saddlebag so I had to leave it on the edge of the road. I got on to head back. God it was steep! The brake lever was bent and mud caked the disc. The brakes had frozen and I couldn't move it. You know how he is. He grabbed the bike, kicked at the dirt encased around the brakes, freed it up and screamed at me to get a fucking grip and ride the bike."

I imagined Jake in his battle frenzy, with tongues of fire on the end of every hair and fists clenched tighter than his jaw.

"Then what?"

"That SOB just left me with my bike running and pointing downhill. He jumped on his Beemer and left. Over his shoulder he shouted, 'No hard feelings!' and tore off. I never saw him again."

"He just left you?"

Nearly spitting, he railed against Jake. "He's not a leader, he's a psychopath. You just don't leave your group and make them fend for themselves. What kind of man does that? You stay with your group! I'm done with him! Dave, do you have any idea why he reacted so strongly to my wreck? Why was he so determined to get on with the trip when it was obviously best to go back? What drives a man like that?"

I dropped some of my psychological BS on him. He wasn't impressed. He needed to spew, not figure things out.

"I don't know man, but if you ever figure it out, let me know. I'm just fucking pissed off! You just don't leave your friends like that!"

Tom kept at his diatribe for a long time. Finally I asked, "What did you do with your bike?"

"Man, with my health problems, there was no way I was going to try to ride it out. Fuck it! I went back to Morelos, found a local policeman, and told him that if he would find me a way out I would give him my BMW. He set me up for the bus that left at 4:00 in the morning."

Although shocked that he'd given his bike away, I completely identified with his decision, "I understand why you gave it away. It was such an awful situation." I repeated what I'd already said so many times, "We never should have been on those roads! Damn it, Tom, you must have been in Morelos close to noon. If I hadn't caught that plane out, we could have figured out how to get out of the Canyon together. We must have missed each other only by a few hours."

"David, you wouldn't believe how pissed off my wife is. She's going to make me sell my Harley as soon as I get back to Canada."

"She must not understand what really happened. If you want me to, I'd be glad to call her to explain why you did what you did."

I did understand how in the middle of the pain and after the trauma of a major crash, a near-death experience, and in his deep fatigue, he too would feel that getting out alive at any price was a bargain. It satisfied a loneliness in me to have him acknowledge the horror we'd both been through. I still suffered a bit for having put them in the awkward position of forging on as a twosome. Most of all I was embarrassed that I'd given away my authority to Jake.

"Tom, where did we go wrong? I've been trying to figure out what blinded us to the part of us that knew better. We both told each other that we didn't want to ride off-road, yet we kept at it. You remember the first night in the tent? I argued to turn back, but both you and Jake refused. We never should have trusted that map. Tom, do you realize that our stubbornness made us stick to the plan regardless of the fact that neither of us wanted the experience we were having?"

"Yeah, but it's like the old story of a frog in a pot of water being heated on a stove. It doesn't jump out because it gets lulled into sleep and ends up being boiled to death. It all happened slowly."

We talked for about an hour trying to ease our pain, sort our confusion, and mollify our grief and trauma. It was comforting to again connect to our deeper parts like we did when we talked in Mazatlán. As if we needed each other's solace we often repeated, "You had to have been there."

"Give me your wife's number and I'll call her to explain the situation from my point of view. You had to have been there to understand why we made the decisions we did."

I called Theresa and tried to convey the magnitude of our desperation and why it made sense to me that Tom would make the decision he did to leave his bike there. I couldn't get her away from her horror that he had given his $11,000 bike away. For her, he was stupid and I imagined that she would make him pay for his "stupidity." Try as much as I could, I was unable to paint a picture vivid enough to soften her judgment. I was unable to have her understand that in those circumstances saving our lives became more important than saving money.

"But listen," I implored, "every fifteen minutes, the road conditions changed. It was impossible to adjust to any one type of road because as soon as we managed our way through one situation, we were met with another new challenge. I have never been so tired and so scared in my whole life. I hope you can find a way to understand how hard it was!"

My words didn't help.

That's the trouble with maps. That's the trouble with communication. Once an internal story seizes the mind, anyone holding a different point of view becomes the enemy and fair game for derision and shame. While talking to her I also recognized my ongoing attempts to justify and understand my own decisions, because the further removed I was from my trauma, the less I understood them myself.

••

I Am as Bad as I Think I Am

Be kind for everyone you meet is fighting a hard battle.

—Ian McLaren

Still trying to work past the stress of the whole ordeal, I ran into Susan in the neighborhood a few weeks later. She'd told me earlier that when Jake got out of the Canyon and into the States he'd decided to continue all the way to Alaska. He'd alluded to his desire to make it all the way to the Arctic Circle, and after arriving in Idaho he turned his BMW north to fulfill his dream. I asked her about his progress, "How's he doing? Has he spoken about his time with Tom and me?" I was really fishing for his feelings about our trip.

"He hasn't said anything about your trip. He took a bunch of pictures and will talk to me about it later."

"Has he ever asked how I was doing?"

"No."

Since I returned I had been doing everything I could to flush all the adrenalin out of my system. I was disappointed that I hadn't heard from him and that he hadn't even asked about my well-being. I had my own resentment for the outcome of the trip, and after Tom dumped all his venom on me I bore the additional weight of his anger as well. I wanted out from under his unfinished rage.

It was convenient for me to unload part of that anger by passing on Tom's rage to Susan. "Jake's gotta know that Tom is furious with him and from what he told me, his relationship with Jake is over!" I was too proud and sophisticated to allow myself to blame him. After all, I made my own decision to ride, my hand was on the throttle.

I felt a familiar elation when I dumped some of my acid by telling her Tom's feelings. I wanted to find someone to blame so I could feel better. I couldn't bring myself to rail against either of them personally or directly because the hard times together had created camaraderie among us that I didn't want to jeopardize.

Susan went on, "I told him if his decision to leave Tom in the Canyon damaged my relationship with Theresa, one of my best friends, I'd never forgive him! Yesterday he got a clue and made a 90-degree turn at Calgary and headed east to Edmonton to square things with Tom. I told him it was now or never to make it right."

"Did they talk?"

She snorted, "You don't know Jake very well! They went out and had a beer and the next day Tom rode his Harley back to Calgary with him. Apparently all is well between them."

"But Tom was so furious he told me he'd never talk to him again."

She just shrugged.

My whole career I'd tried to help men learn that life works better if they acknowledge their feelings and work things out. Obviously Tom was furious with Jake for leaving him in a lurch. When Tom and I talked on the phone I told him that he needed to talk with Jake to work out his anger or else their relationship would never be the same. He reacted, "Hell, I'm not angry. Fuck him, I just think he's a psychopath and he never should have left me in the Canyon. You just don't do that when you ride together. None of my friends would even dream about leaving someone alone. They all think he must be crazy. I will never talk to him again, but no, I'm not angry."

I'm wired differently. I need to talk things through to clear them up, and my anger, if unaddressed, simmers or freezes and comes out distorted later. If I didn't talk this through, my friendship with Jake would probably end. I didn't want that.

Jake was gone for a month and a half on his trip to Alaska. When he returned from the Arctic Circle, I anticipated he would immediately give me a call to talk about all we'd been through and to tell me the stories about the rest of his trip. His single-mindedness impressed me. I wanted to live vicariously through his 14,000-mile journey through three countries, see his pictures, hear his adventures and most of all, talk to him about our time together in the Canyon.

Nothing came my way from him while he was on his trip. I wanted him to call, thinking that all we'd been through would drive him to at least e-mail me or send some pictures. When I first saw him in the neighborhood, I rushed up and asked him about his trip.

"I made it all the way to the Arctic Circle. I took off my shoes and dipped my toes into that cold water. I did 14,000 miles!" He told me a few stories but the icy air between us remained.

"Let's get together and talk about the trip later," and I excused myself.

This frigidity stayed between us for some time. If he saw me he would abruptly turn away and head back into his house. In part I wanted to retaliate against Jake, but most of all I needed to talk about the trip, compare stories, perceptions, and internal struggles. I hadn't yet untangled my unfinished feelings, some of which were Tom's and some my own. Finally one day when I could contain myself no longer, I called him, "Jake, I want to get together and talk about our trip. A bunch of crap came down and I'd like to understand more about that."

"Hey, come on up. We'll have a beer and talk."

I'd heard Tom's version of the crash and the fight that sent them on their separate ways. I still carried Tom's anger and judgment and was weighed down by the burden of his unfinished business. Knowing how we all distort stories to justify ourselves, I wanted to hear it from Jake's perspective as well.

I came right out and asked the hard question, "What happened between you and Tom?"

He shook his head, "It was awful, Dave. When we left Morelos I had at least half of Tom's gear on my bike. Remember he broke his saddlebag bracket. We stopped to buy some water and orange soda at the little store not far away from our hotel.

God, that hotel was a dive."

"Did you buy any real food?"

"No. There wasn't much there that would travel well. They didn't have any Pop Tarts!"

"Yeah, you bought food for a king." We laughed. "I still can't believe that Pop Tarts was your food of choice. When my driver roared out of town to meet the airplane, I saw you guys stuffing the bottles under your straps."

"And that's really where all the trouble started, because two hours up the road we had to cross another river. On the way up the other side, his last bottle bounced off his bike. I told him he should go back and pick it up because he was going to need it later on."

"Tom said, Fuck it. I'll pick some up at the next town. I'm not riding back down to get it.'

"A little later, we headed up a very steep, deeply rutted hill, and Tom went down HARD. When I got up to him, he was still lying on his back, 10 or 15 feet in front of his bike. I guess he flipped over the handlebars. I checked his tire tracks and they were four inches from the edge of a 1,000 foot drop-off!"

Jake went on, "You know I'm terrified of heights, right, and looking down that cliff gave me the heebie-jeebies." He shuddered involuntarily. "I couldn't get any closer to the cliff and told him we had to pull the bike back into the middle of the road. FOUR INCHES from that cliff!" He shut his eyes and shuddered again.

His eyes widened and he repeated every syllable two or three times. "FOUR INCHES! FOUR FUCKING INCHES! God, I hate heights!"

"How'd that happen?" I asked, trying to get a picture to understand why he flipped.

"The ruts," he put his hands in front of him about 16 inches apart, "were this deep. I looked back down the hill and saw the big rock he ran into that sent him up to the left into the hillside. He bounced against the wall that sent him back across the road straight towards the cliff. His front tire dropped into the rut and he must have been thrown over the handlebars. He was only inches away from that huge drop. God, it was scary. If his tire hadn't jammed in the rut he would have gone straight over the ledge! Just remembering looking down the cliff still gives me the shivers." His body shook again.

"It's weird, Jake, but that entire day I had this ominous feeling and special fear for you guys, especially Tom. From the plane I could see how steep the roads were. My god, he must have been scared shitless."

"Four inches from the cliff. FOUR FUCKING INCHES! I hate heights!"

His repetition told me that he was trying to flush his own trauma. I raised my eyebrows and nodded for him to continue.

"We sat down on the edge of the road. I took a drink. He looked at me, obviously thirsty and I offered him a sip. He put it up to his lips and started chugging away. 'Hey,' I yelled, 'are you going to chug the whole thing? That's all I have! You left yours down the hill.' He just stared at me for a minute and then he leaned back and finished the whole bottle. Pissed me off big time!

"Then, AFTER he drained it all he told me, 'I'm not going on. I'm going back to Morelos. Ride back with me.' Fuck that shit. You just drank my last water and you want me to ride back two hours to Morelos. If you think I am going back just to have to come up through this section of road again, you're crazy! Who is going to ride with me for the next 240 miles without any water? What am I going to drink the rest of the day?"

Jake looked at me defiantly, pleading, "Shit, man, what was I supposed to do? I told him, 'Fuck it, if you aren't going on, then let's get your bike turned around so I can get on with my trip.' He grabbed my empty bottle and threw it over the cliff!" Jake was in near fury as he told me his version.

"Why didn't you turn around with him?" I asked.

"Are you shitting me? I had a goal to get to Alaska and wasn't going to let anything get in my way!"

I remembered how the sparks flew when we were in Barra de Navidad arguing about politics. I could imagine these two belligerent men bellowing chest to chest, index fingers poking into each other's faces, having it out.

My gut clenched with the same tightness I experienced whenever I remembered his impatience to get back on the road. The pressure to push on started from the beginning of our trip when he and Tom didn't bother getting insurance because they were in too much of a hurry to leave. I wondered where this urgency came from.

"He got on his bike and the brakes wouldn't work because they were all goobered up with mud from the crash. The foot brake was bent and the front brake lever wouldn't pull. I dug the mud away from the brake calipers, straightened his pedal, and screamed at him to get on the fucking bike, give it some gas, and go on back to Morelos."

As he explained the difficulties of getting Tom and the bike ready to return, I wanted to hear some compassion or understanding that Tom was obviously in shock, in pain, and most importantly terrified not only of getting back on the bike again, but of traveling alone in his state for the two-hour drive back to Morelos. It takes time to recover from a crash like that and I identified with his being on that lonely ride back down to the village at the bottom of the Canyon. I wanted to understand how Jake could rationalize leaving him there. Was he a sociopath as Tom wanted to believe or was he driven by something I couldn't see?

"What about his gear?"

"He reorganized some of it and had to leave one of his saddlebags alongside the road. I sure as hell wasn't going to pack it to Canada for him!"

I mentioned Jake's e-mail that Susan forwarded to me after he got out of the Canyon and spent the night in Creel. "You said you had no food or water for two and a half days, 115-degree heat, and had to strip the bike completely to get out. Tell me about it."

In that e-mail, he'd written a line that really bothered me, "I am as bad as I think I am..." The arrogance in that message ticked me off because at that point his "victorious" trip out had also resulted in disasters for both Tom and me. *Why would he say that? Where was his remorse or sense of shared responsibility for the outcome for all of us? What was he trying to prove?* I wanted some understanding of that or else I didn't think I would ever want to spend time with him again. I also wondered about his exaggeration, as if he couldn't acknowledge his own terror.

He went on to tell me some of the scary times he had while alone. "The road I was on forced me down this incredibly steep and crumbly section. I knew that if I started down, I wouldn't be able to turn around. At the bottom I discovered that the recent rains had washed out the bridge. In order to cross the river and get to the other side I had to pop a wheelie at the edge of the stream to get the front wheel up and over the 40-inch bank. When the front wheel cleared the lip I threw my body forward and pulled the bike with me." Jake stood up and showed me the way he had to contort his body to get over the edge.

"As soon as I cleared the lip and headed up the road, the bike spun around and turned back towards the river again, and I crashed headed the wrong way. The road was too slippery to drive any further and I had no idea how I was going to turn it 180 degrees to climb the hill. While I was figuring out how to get going again, the rain started. I set up camp and waited for two days in the rain without food or water before I could move."

Jake then told me about how his fear of ever getting out brought on a crisis of faith. In the hours spent in the tent alone, hungry, scared, and without water, he began to read a Bible a friend had given him. "The morning the rain stopped, I unzipped the tent I'd pitched in the road, stood up, and stretched in the sunshine. I jumped back in fright when I saw two short dark men staring at me from the edge of the road. They were wearing a loincloth kind of thing and sandals. They seemed friendly. I signaled with my hand to indicate that I'd dumped my bike and needed to turn it around. Together the three of us picked it up, turned it around, and got it headed uphill. I wanted a picture, but by the time I found my camera, they'd disappeared."

"My gosh, that must have been amazing for them! I wonder how long they'd been watching you and what they must have thought when this big black man crawled out of a huge bright green tent. Who knows, maybe you were a new god in their eyes."

These men were the legendary Tarahumara, among the few remaining indigenous tribes unconquered by the Spaniards. The Spanish had slaughtered, robbed, and raped all of Mexico, but here in the Canyon, this most resilient tribe had been left alone because they were too much trouble to subdue. Tarahumara are well known for their ability to thrive in the remote canyons, and are especially famous for their capacity to run for miles up and down slopes with only thin leather sandals on their feet. Men and women alike have been ultradistance runners as far back as time knows. Their legs were their sole transportation.

"After we turned the bike around it was still too steep to get moving on the disintegrated granite road. I decided that the only way out was to strip the bike down to nothing and pack my gear up and out of this Canyon. I carried it all by hand, including my seat, at least a half-mile up that road. I could then straddle my bike and walk/ride my way out. The temp gauge on my bike read 117 degrees!"

I marveled at his resolve. I couldn't help but wonder what I would have done if I'd found myself in that situation. Would I have had the same resilience if my life depended on it? I'd bailed out of the Canyon before it got that horrendous. I shuddered because I would not have wanted to have to answer that challenge, but Jake relied on his ability to attack everything and never lose. Something drove him that didn't drive me!

With a desire to shift the conversation to a more personal note I offered, "For me, Jake, I didn't and don't have the need to go on beyond what is safe for me. I'll test my edge but I know when I've reached the limit of what I can or want to do, and it's not a signal of defeat when I come to that place where I say 'enough!'"

His reply shocked me, "I've never understood the idea of limitation. Last night I watched a TV program and it described different situations where people came to the end of what they could do." He screwed up his face in genuine confusion. "I've never found that place in me that says 'I quit.' I've never taken on anything I couldn't beat and I never will. There is no quit in me, but I thought about you and Tom last night when I watched Magnum Force and heard something I'd never understood before. 'Every man has his limits.' I thought to myself, maybe Dave and Tom simply reached their limit." The realization that Tom and I had reached our limits seemed to help him drop his judgments.

"But Jake," I challenged, "what if you're in a life and death situation, surely you'd turn back."

"Absolutely not! I'd rather die! Seriously, if I died trying something I'd started, at least I'd go out knowing I gave it my all and I'd die without any regrets."

As he spoke I had to acknowledge that he indeed lived his life that way, throwing himself into every adventure 100 percent. This helped me understand his e-mail, "I am as bad as I think I am." He HAD to be tough. His identity surrounded the idea that he would or could never back down. A great difference appeared between us because I have found great personal power when I have pressed against my limits and then admitted where I'm inadequate or vulnerable. I've lost my need to prove that I'm not scared, but Jake found comfort in his ability to conquer anything he'd started.

We'd been talking about his version of the trip for nearly an hour, but I wasn't satisfied. He asked me nothing about my trip out, my tangles with the insurance company, nor how I made it out. My interest in his trip was genuine but I was miffed that he didn't return the courtesy of reciprocal curiosity. I tried to get him inside my experience. "You're an incredible rider! I cannot imagine what it must have been like. My trip has been a journey in itself. In addition to my rib problem, I lost most of my riding gear and I've been in a frustrating battle with the insurance company! They're absolutely incompetent. I struggled for awhile with the feeling of having been abandoned in Morelos."

He exploded, "What in the fuck are you talking about? You fucking abandoned me! I was there in the wild with no one to talk to, no food, no water, soaking in the rain! How dare you talk about being abandoned! I was all alone!"

A medicine ball had just been dropped on my chest. I was nearly knocked off the stool by that accusation. I'd touched a 10,000-volt nerve. When I finally was able to get out of my shock I glared at him, "I was hurt! I had a bike that wouldn't run! I had to find my own way out. I was alone in that god-forsaken village. How did I abandon you?"

His voice came out staccato, every spitting word carefully separated for emphasis. His eyes narrowed and with a ferocity I've rarely seen in a man as he lunged at my face as if he was saying something he'd never admitted to himself, "You don't have a FUCKING CLUE about being alone! You've never been alone!"

"You've never asked me about my life. How in the hell would you know?"

His neck flared like a cobra, "I've been alone every day of my entire life. I went to school and was the only black kid in an Amish town and every day I had to fight bigger kids than myself. To keep me from getting my ass kicked my father bought a pair of boxing gloves, took me to the ring and knocked me around until I learned how to defend myself. Then when I beat up my classmates, they would send bigger brothers and I took them all on, one by one. I never lost a fight. That was my life and I never quit."

He paused and moved down from that cliff-edge of rage. His voice softened. His eyes almost in grief and his remorse apparent, "Damn it, Dave, if we had stayed together we all could have made it! Three together can do anything!"

"But, Jake" I repeated, "I couldn't ride and my bike wouldn't run. You tried to start it. There is no way I could've spent another day on the road. Tom was in shock and had come to his limits as well."

"I read a story about a guy who broke his leg and he was deep in the jungle. He used his shoelaces to tie his leg around a stick and drove out anyway. You just can't quit once you get started!"

I'd obviously touched something at his essential core. "Sorry, I'd reached my limit. I would not go on and I didn't need to further jeopardize my life."

After he'd sprayed all over me, it seemed like he'd just put a ghost behind him. Then a bit more interested in dialogue he acknowledged with pride, "I've never quit anything. To turn back means that I am a complete failure. I will never turn back from what I started." He repeated what he said before. "If I die trying, then everyone will know that I lived with absolutely no regrets."

Suddenly I realized that the knife at his back that had been pushing Jake, his drive, his impatience, his menacing fierceness, and dangerous commitment to keeping himself from ever turning back, came from the terror of a little boy who would have been unmercifully shamed if he ever let down, ever cried, ever let the racist bullies find out that he was scared. It would have meant that he had failed. He answered the challenge of ridicule by being ferocious, and for that ferocity he was proud.

A veil immediately lifted for me when I saw not a belligerent, calloused, and selfish man, but a man caught by a lifelong, viciously protective voice that insisted, "If you turn back, you're a loser." At his core, a life and death battle against shame. He had been backed into a corner time and time again by a racist world and he responded with an ethic dedicated to never showing weakness, never being conquered, and never giving in to fear lest he betray his total life essence. He was as "bad" as he thought he was. To stay alive he put his life at risk.

All of a sudden, his decision to go his own way, to set a course and not deviate from it, no longer seemed right or wrong to me. I understood his map. When the ferocity of his survival story touched my heart, forgiveness swept over me despite all I'd held against him. It was a forgiveness that grew not out of any magnanimity but out of something a philosopher had said, "Be kind, for everyone you meet is fighting a great battle."

••

The Mordida

We have met the enemy and the enemy is us. —**Pogo**

Although I'd left my bike, never expecting to see it or even ride again, it didn't take long before Gloria and I began in earnest to attempt to retrieve it. A week after I signed my insurance claim in Chihuahua I became increasingly concerned because I hadn't heard from insurance adjuster Ramón. The longer I didn't hear from him the more my agitation grew. I began calling him with increasing frequency. He never answered. Finally I went over his head in the chain of command and talked to his supervisor asking with thinly veiled irritation if he had any information regarding the progress of retrieving my bike. He remembered my situation because Gloria had talked to him while I was in Guachochi. He had no information and promised to get back to me as soon as he knew something. I waited days, sent several emails but didn't hear back.

A full month after I wrecked, I finally got the supervisor on the phone, "*Señor* Bryen, I am sorry to tell you that Ramón is no longer working with us. He left three weeks ago and we haven't heard from him since."

"Where's my bike? Where's the key I left for him?"

"We don't know but we will send an adjuster to the town to find it. Where is this town of Morelos?"

The supervisor gave me the name of another adjuster who would take over the case. I was back to square one with no idea of where the bike was now, or if it had ever been found or fixed. I lived with a constant nagging in my gut, fearing it had been stolen for sure. Several weeks passed and various agents assured me that it had been hauled out and was in Guachochi, now in Parral, now in Chihuahua. Finally I got it straight from the supervisor for gringo claims in Mexico, "*Señor* Bryen, I now have to tell you that no one has seen the bike."

"Has anyone gone into the Canyon to find it?"

"No, you need to fill out an insurance report because Ramón never turned one in. We have no record of the accident and you didn't file a police report."

"But there was no reason to file a police report; I only needed to use the Travel Assistance I paid for in my insurance!" All my politeness was gone.

By now, in early August, the rainy season was in full swing and the roads, even for the natives, were impassable. It took the insurance company another three weeks to get an adjuster to come to my house to make the second report.

When I asked the supervisor how long it would take to get into the Canyon and get the bike out he skirted my question, "It's impossible now to get into that area. The roads are all washed out."

It became clear to me somewhere in the middle of my frustration that my American insistence, my American intensity, my American threats, and the force of my fierce personality were completely ineffectual in Mexico. In subsequent calls I realized that the insurance personnel, rather than being up front and telling me what they did or didn't know, would simply become passive, put me on hold, or be called away on more important business. *"Mañana"* means "not today" or more accurately "I don't know." It is deemed socially incorrect to say "I don't know." This culture teaches that it's better to give a story of hope, even if it's completely wrong, than disappoint someone by not offering anything.

I would wait for hours sometimes while a series of insurance agents would come to the phone and ask me whom I wanted to talk to. Meanwhile the supervisor had gone home, out to lunch, or was called to an important meeting. For them, my bike was just a troublesome case, but for me it was a treasure I wanted to reclaim. I tried in vain to pull someone out of the institutional woodwork to take personal interest in my case.

Gradually, in the interminable waiting game with the insurance company, I gave up my previous methods of intimidation and learned that I could find inner peace even while waiting on the phone, listening to endless repetitions of a computer generated "Yellow Rose of Texas." My hurry-up, obsessive sense of time left me in favor of a calm that allowed me to enjoy the present even when the fate of my motorcycle was uncertain. I'd been living with the illusion that time was at a premium and I needed immediate resolution to feel peace again. Whereas before I'd constantly felt the pressure of time as if I were caught underwater and needed to rise quickly for air, my new calmness allowed me to stay on the phone without impatience or anger. Something released and I embraced the concept of mañana, realizing that retirement for me offered an opportunity to step out of time-bound anxiety.

We learned on a trip to Thailand years ago that the Thai's response when foreigners insisted on a clear commitment to finish a job was to say "Not yes, not no." It's an eloquent answer to the obsession for timeliness. It simply offers the option that suggests that the time is not ripe, or I am not ready to give an opinion or make a decision. It offers both client and provider a way to wait until the right time comes. Lao Tzu asked, "Do you have the patience to wait till the mud settles and the water is clear? Can you remain unmoving till the right action arises by itself?"

Meanwhile I was not totally patient and started looking on Craig's List for a bike to replace the one that was surely lost in the Canyon. In late September, three months after I wrecked, we got word from the Canyon. The insurance adjuster had a cousin who lived in Guachochi that had a friend in Morelos who had seen someone riding my motorcycle. A supervisor who had finally taken personal interest in my case began pressuring his contacts in Morelos to find the bike. The social networks in the bowels of the remote canyons are like a spider web in which people know what is happening in every corner of their world. I answered the phone one day to hear, "*Señor* Bryen, we talked to the doctor in Morelos and he told us that you gave him your bike in exchange for healing your rib. Therefore my boss has denied your claim and you won't get any money from us."

My patience exhausted, I erupted, "I never saw a doctor! I never gave my bike to anyone. I simply left the bike in the mechanic's yard! My friend gave his BMW to the local authorities. You're confusing two stories. The doctor is lying to you! I demand that the insurance company reconsider their decision!"

Two days later he called me again, "My superiors at the insurance company said you will have to go back into Morelos to talk to the doctor and settle this with him."

By this time, I'd rounded up some local Mexican friends who were willing to fly up there to help me, so I said, "I will buy a ticket tomorrow and fly up there with my friends and talk to this so-called Doctor!" My boldness and willingness to immediately fly up there to go back to Morelos must have set them back. I'd called their bluff. In two hours they called me again and said they had made a new determination. A drug lord had threatened people there and because of the danger to me if I were to go to Morelos to settle matters, they would indeed consider it a stolen bike and reimburse me for my loss. "You must go to the insurance office in Guadalajara and sign the title and registration over to us and we will pay you for the stolen bike."

On Thursday in the last week of September, I drove into Guadalajara to sign my title and registration over to the insurance company. Still mistrustful of the insurance company that had been so inefficient in processing my claim and equally skeptical of the Mexican law, they assured me, "No problem, Señor, the deposit will be in your bank in a few days." I just signed my bike away and no longer had any legal right to it. Their payment of $2,400 was very different from the $6,000 the bike was worth, but by that time I felt lucky that I'd ever see any money at all.

I was relieved that it had finally been settled. However, the very next day I got another call, "Señor Bryen, they just found your bike in someone's garage in Guachochi, not in Morelos as we thought! It's there, it's undamaged. We have not processed the papers and if you want your old bike back you can have it. Because you have signed the title to us you can have the money or the bike, you decide."

"You're kidding me! Before I make that decision, can you send me a picture of the bike? How will I know if they've trashed it riding on those roads?"

"My friend's friend says your bike's OK. I'll send you pictures."

The next day they sent several pictures over and sure enough, there she was, and as far as I could tell from the grainy cell phone photo, it was my precious Suzi, dirty, but just as I'd left her!

Later the supervisor called again. "We've run into another problem. The drug lord who has the bike wants 15,000 pesos to release it. It's up to you, what do you want to do?"

"Those sons-a-bitches!" I yelled in Gloria's direction. "You won't believe the next round in Mexico's incompetency. A drug lord wants a 15,000-peso *mordida* ($1,200 USD) for me to get it back! I can't believe it! I've got a few days to figure out if I will accept a check for the total loss of $2,400 or pay $1,200 just to get it back. By the way, did you know *mordida* means "bite?"

In the meantime, shortly after they'd told me earlier that I would be given a payment for the stolen bike, I'd gone online and finished the money transfer to buy a similar motorcycle in California. It was sitting in the former owner's garage in California. I now owned two identical bikes. After I did the math I figured that it would be far cheaper to pay the $1200 and repair any damage than to drive to California, pay more for the new bike, and equip it for riding in Mexico. I told the insurance company, "Tell the drug dealer that I'll pay the *mordida* but I won't be wiring the money and will bring it up in person. I won't pay a dime until I have the motorcycle in my possession."

The challenge for me was to figure out how to face the drug lord without his taking my money, chopping off my head, and riding off on my motorcycle. "Can you find some people who will help me make the exchange so I don't get robbed or killed?"

"Oh, yes," the supervisor assured me, "we can make the exchange at our office in Parral."

Although I'd come to a rational financial decision, I was still grousing about the slippery morality of Mexico, the insurance company, and the adjusters that were in bed with the known criminal element. A few days after that in a coffee shop on the shores of Lake Chapala, I sat with another motorcycle rider bitching about my resentment toward Mexican corruption and the required mordida. "How dare they stick me for $1,200 to get my bike back!"

Then a layer of fog lifted and I came face to face with my own immature sense of "they owe me." I'd made the choice to ride my bike where I shouldn't have gone, on a motorcycle not equipped for the kind of riding required there, without proper preparation and equipment, useless maps, and lack of group cohesion. I was the one who wrecked my bike and hurried out of the Canyon before making adequate arrangements to get the bike out. Even though the insurance company had been incompetent and inefficient, I had to look at how I bungled my own affairs. Had I been given the option of spending $1,200 to get the bike out of the Canyon four months ago, I would have gladly paid the money. Was I complaining about the cost because a bandit demanded it? Or did my objection come from hurt pride that someone had me by the short hairs and had intimidated me? Shouldn't it have been enough that I'd bought an insurance policy?

Like most gringos who come to Mexico, I'd struggled with the functional reality of the bribery system. When it came to dealing with traffic violations I'd accepted the way the local police padded their meager salaries by taking pesos in lieu of issuing a ticket. On a larger scale, however, the political corruption the *mordida* encouraged seemed at the root of a broken judicial system. Money under the table seemed to be the overt method of clearing criminals of deserved jail time. It keeps the rich and dishonest in power. Money and corruption seemed to go hand in hand but I didn't know if the rural Mexicans had as much moral repugnancy for it as I did. This was especially true for those doing business in the remote Canyon. I was not in a position to judge the insurance company for acquiescing in the drug lord's demand for my money. The retrieval of my bike was fraught with difficulties of impassable roads, spotty cell phone service, and unreliable information.

I found some clarity, however, when I realized that my own angry reaction was more like a child in a temper tantrum whining because he or she wasn't being treated fairly. I expected to be treated with the same kind of justice I'd learned to expect in the United States. I'd assumed the insurance company would take care of my mistakes, get my bike out of the Canyon, and restore my sense of wholeness. Though the insurance company was agonizingly inefficient, I could no longer blame them because the conditions of the Canyon made it nearly impossible to find my motorcycle and haul it out.

Even though I'd made a decision based on my financial benefit, I will remember forever the impact of the insight that swept over me while talking to my friend. Like walking into the kind of clarity that comes when the sun shines after a long and dark storm, a new map replaced the old one. "For me, it's all about the shadow," I explained to my friend. "It's easy to condemn the incompetence of the insurance company and turn my anger at them, when the real issue is my struggle with myself for my errors of judgment."

He held up his hand to slow me down, "Whoa. What do you mean 'shadow'?"

"Shadow basically means we are blind to our own foibles and condemn those same foibles in others that we have not reconciled inside ourselves. If I've not come to terms with my weakness, I'll condemn it in others; if I don't deal with my fear, I'll judge anyone who is fearful. Most emotion-laden conflict can be resolved if individuals can see their own blind spots."

Maybe it was a way for me to wrestle with my lingering feelings of inadequacy but when I saw my own contradictions, I went on. "It's only right for me to pay something to those who found my bike and are working to get it out. The insurance company is not my mother!"

I went on, "In the United States, we have the idea that insurance is an industry that makes a contract with its clients to repair or repay for loss or damage. But we've expanded this idea to mean that we are supposed to get bailed out from the consequences of our choices. This expectation has crept unchallenged into our culture." Shifting gears, I went on, "When we ride our motorcycles, we have to assume full responsibility for the decisions we make. If the person leading a ride takes a risk and others follow, it's not the leader's fault if someone behind has an accident. You know as a rider that one of the first lessons you learn when riding in a group is to ride your own ride. Ride within your limits. Any expectations to have others save your ass when you make a mistake has no place in motorcycle riding and, as far as I can see, it's a cancerous idea that needs to be brought forward in public consciousness.

When Gloria and I decided to move here we accepted the challenges Mexico would bring and tried to be aware that frustrations and inefficiencies would be part of our experience. Nonetheless, we chose to move here and accept the challenges that come along with that. Here we don't expect the roads to be pristine, or institutions and services to be predictable, and living here requires fresh adaption to new challenges each day.

My trip to the Canyon had knocked me off center but now I'd returned to a clearer place. With this homecoming I took a deep breath and seriously thought I'd be quickly rewarded with a returned bike.

However, the insurance supervisor, apparently intimidated

by the violent potential of meeting the drug lord called me and reported, "We gave the *bandito* your message that you would be bringing the money up to Guachochi in exchange for the bike, but he said that the insurance company took too long to get the information so he would no longer cooperate. He is going to keep the bike." In the meantime I'd driven into Guadalajara to retrieve the title I'd signed over but they hadn't filed. The insurance adjuster said, "We are sorry to say that now you must please go back to Guadalajara and again sign the title over to us. We will pay you what we agreed."

The money came into my bank account just as they said. Being unfamiliar with Mexican law, I thought it would be easy to get my stolen bike off its temporary immigration permit so I would be allowed to bring in the replacement bike I'd just bought in California. However, the process of getting the official police report was fraught with yet another round of Mexican inefficiencies. Just in time, six months after I wrecked the Suzuki, we managed to secure the official report at the Border station in Nogales on our way to California to pick up my new bike. We crossed the Border with our report in hand, sure that our ordeal was over. We'd driven over 2,000 miles north and returned to the Border towing the new bike, expecting to have our stolen bike's temporary import permit removed from the system. It was then we learned that we couldn't import the new bike. According to Mexico's records, I already had a bike in the country, and although it had been stolen, I was not allowed by Mexican law to bring in another one. In order to bring in the new bike, we had to first go through a very complicated legal process that would take months.

Nearly six months after I crashed the bike, we sat at the Border wondering what to do. With tears of absolute frustration streaming down Gloria's face, I said, "Fuck it," and brought the new bike across illegally

••

The Water Seeks the Thirsty

Not only the thirsty seek the water, the water as well seeks the thirsty.

—Rumi

Uncertainty greets anyone who endeavors to step out of the ordinary. However, allegiance to the ordinary also serves as a defense against feeling the built-in anxiety that comes along with our fate as human beings. Jung reminded us, "Deep down, below the surface of the average man's conscience, he hears a voice whispering, 'There is something not right,' no matter how much his rightness is supported by public opinion or moral code." Jake, Tom and I, along with most of the motorcyclists I've ever known, shared a desire to get off the couch, experience the freedom of the open road, connect to our badassness, and act out a bit of our inner outlaw.

Elemental parts of our connection to the world have been suffocated by cultural civility and we have an aversion to the cushioned comfort of traveling in a metal cage where everything we see is just like boring TV. An independent spirit howls for recognition and expression. On a motorcycle the protection is gone and you're not just watching the world, you're completely in contact with it. You're in the world and the sense of presence is overwhelming. We know that we cannot experience life in our maps or in our books.

While in the Canyon and in my own struggles after I returned, various facets of my personality surfaced the way a carbonated drink keeps sending bubbles to the top. During the trip's ordeal, one part of me was simply terrified and wanted to go home. This scared part continually reminded me of my pain and pulled my attention off the road in order to have me imagine every possible catastrophe. Another part, wearing a bolder, proud mask didn't want to chicken out and leave the others. I was mostly afraid of being condemned for being weak or cowardly, and knew I would be my own worst critic after I was safe at home. The writer/poet in me had fantasized about conquering the Canyon and making it all the way so I could return to write and thump my chest holding the bloody scalps of fear and cowardice in my raised and victorious fist. I wanted pictures and treasures and big stories to tell. The lifelong lover of all things motorcycle thrilled at the visceral experience of seeing, learning, and traveling in this astounding country. I was pleased that I'd taken on this adventure.

At times I feel my true identity is more like a drop of water dancing on top of hot oil, trying to find a place to land. Consciousness is like that. Without awareness, true essence bounces around homeless, looking for a place to land. But every now and then the aspect of my personality that looks at me when I am looking in the mirror takes over. This ancient part of me lives outside of my emotional dissonance and is amused at how much I fuss with "stuff." This detached witness simply observes all of what I am going through and, unlike the less developed parts of my personality, never clamors for recognition. It just sits back in the easy chair available to me whenever I have the sense to shift to its wisdom. This objective One standing above all my drama is the home I continually long for.

Inside our heads there is a witness that watches our thoughts, offering an almost omniscient perspective on who we are and where we are going. The *One Who Is Aware* cooperates with fate or destiny as if it is a weaver who over time creates a tapestry of the particulars of my life embedded with purpose and meaning. When I am in the reflective times of life I look back and see the wisdom of all the bridges I've crossed. Without adequate words to describe the intricacies of life's tapestry, Wordsworth referred to it as "a dark invisible workmanship that reconciles discordant elements and makes them move in one society." It's the map we find when we ride off the edge of our current map. It's the turtle that stands on the back of another turtle, all the way down.

The one who is aware is the one who recognizes that the map is only a temporary guide that better serves mankind if held lightly. Whenever I manage to access it, its calming, witnessing perspective allows me to simply rest in life itself. To find what supports me when all my maps, stories, beliefs and strategies don't work anymore is the greatest treasure of life. When Jung pointed out "underneath, something is not right," he was talking about our disconnection to this aspect of our being. To find our way to that equanimity is the quintessential human search. The way to that place is by embracing the fact that doubt and insecurity are indispensable components of a complete life.

The Old Architect who came to me years ago announcing that he was the one who built all the bridges I'd ever crossed, was an image given to me in a dream. The image and the presence behind the image lived beyond any map I could see, but nevertheless it wanted a relationship with me and needed my help. This wisdom seeks us! I like the German poet Rilke's way to explore the meaning of our life. He said that we are "a habit that discovered us, found us comfortable, and moved in." Our lives require coming to terms with whatever it is that is trying to find us so it can move in. Jung referred to this when he said that to find what supports us when all else fades away is the highest and best experience we will ever have in life.

I happened into this experience once when I did my first skydive with our son in South Africa. I was clipped to Julian, the skydive master. "When the door rolls back, fold your arms across your chest and as soon as our bodies clear the airplane, look up!" he yelled in my ear above the noise of the wind and the airplane.

"How many times have you done this?" I hollered back.

"More than 700, all of them successful!"

We enjoyed each other's banter as we circled, climbing to 9,000 feet above Cape Town. It was a spectacular day. The pristine waters of South Africa, the white sand beaches, and the unpopulated coast stretched before us. Finally at altitude, I watched as Calvin and his tandem dive master scooted on their butts to the door and got sucked out into thin air, immediately vanishing from sight. Suddenly I was forced to the door with my feet dangling off the edge of this tiny plane. I gasped briefly when I looked down, trying to catch my breath in the 120-mph wind that wanted to rip off my T-shirt. There was nothing between terra firma and me.

What happened next was immediate. For a brief moment I hung upside down and the world spun below me. While still hanging upside down, the magic release happened. I didn't create it. The part of me that had been forever holding me up let go and I stopped carrying the weight of my life. All my mental fussing was gone and I rested in something much greater. I sensed everything directly without the interference of thought and I became untethered to myself and a new level of awareness overtook me. Nothing mattered at that moment! Mind got bypassed and no thoughts got in my way. I was aware of nothing other than the experience. I was the bright garden where the senses enlarge and experience the world directly without thought. I became a throat-ripping scream of joy, knowing instantly through experience what it means to live without attachment to outcome.

When I got back to ground, all I could talk about was that exquisite moment when I no longer used my energy to carry my life. I knew in an instant that this is what it is to live each moment as the only moment in history.

This perspective, although not successfully achieved often enough while I struggled in the Canyon, nevertheless points me towards how I should live. If only I can develop the muscle of awareness, I can draw from and live the wisdom that lies outside of my mind and outside of what I have learned. It's the understanding that at all times we are invited to rest deeper and deeper in the guiding sense the "dark invisible workmanship" provides.

In the end, riding off the edge of the map is simply a metaphor for a way to move to a more meaningful life. It happens when we allow ourselves to move from the small familiar map we've come to rely on to the larger map underneath and then jump to the one under that. It is advancing belief into visceral trust, from ideas of the ego into the momentum of the mystery that seeks to manifest itself through our lives. It is finally finding a way to our own contract with life and becoming the portal through which the new finds expression. In riding or living, there is no such thing as balance, only constant opportunities for adjustment.

••

Epilogue

There is no such thing as balance, only constant opportunities for adjustment.
—Daniel Villaseñor

From the airplane flying out of Morelos, I got a taste of the Canyon's grandeur. But the glimpse didn't take care of the hole inside me. After I returned to Ajijic and had bought another bike, I found my way to a compatible bunch of motorcycle riders and began to enjoy time with Jake again. I took many rides across the spectacular Mexican Sierra Madres and rode to some of Mexico's many beaches. I rode on some more awful dirt roads and on pavement but my heart still yearned to settle into what I'd missed in the Canyon.

In the end, my deep regret about the motorcycle adventure was not that I'd abandoned the trip or lost the bike to the drug lord and an inept insurance company, or that my bank account took a hit. It wasn't even in the physical pain I endured or my hurt pride. The failure that haunted me was not having reached that place on the rim of the Canyon where I could kiss and be kissed by its majesty. My longing to get to the Canyon ate at me like a cancer. While it was spectacular to have seen it from the airplane, I missed bathing in all it had to offer. The kind of immersion I wanted would take time, long, delicious, velvety time, sitting on the edge at sunset, watching the sun etch its shadow across the Canyon walls.

On my way out of the Canyon, I'd been rescued by a gracious young man and aided with medication from a lovely *señora*, and even though I got caught by my fear and fled Morelos, I regretted that I hadn't given the people there more of a chance to help me, allowing me to become human and real with them. I wished I'd slowed down, related to the local people rather than use my resources to buy my way out. Because I was afraid, I missed a rare opportunity to deepen my understanding.

It wasn't long before my fear dropped away and like a fire

that never went out, my desire to go to the Canyon rekindled. I had to find a way to get my family there. Over time in our 38-year marriage, each of us has been able to develop the parts of our natural personalities that round out the other, allowing both to experience more than either would have been able alone. Gloria's balance to my spontaneous and sometimes catastrophic adventuring comes in her ability and patience to plan, inquire, and make advanced reservations. Over the years we'd learned how to follow the ideas that come to either one of us, plant these ideas in the fertile space between us, and work with our individual capacities to bring them to fruition. We shared the same vision of visiting the Canyon's pinnacles that spurred Jake, Tom, and me to plan the trip in the first place.

Nearly two years after my motorcycle misadventure, we flew our son Calvin down from Oregon and rendezvoused with him in Mazatlán. We stayed in the same beach hotel where Tom and I had shared the stories that dissolved the strain between us. My family and I sat at the same table eating breakfast, listening to the swoosh of the waves and watching the malecón fill with early morning joggers and people walking their dogs. The layers of my memory rolled across my mind like waves sweeping onto the sand. Observing the far-off look in my eye, Gloria asked, "What are you thinking about?"

"I'm retracing my trip. Everything we talked about here is coming back. I remember the amazing shift in my relationship with Tom after I told him the heron story. I'm feeling so much more comfortable knowing where we are staying, what to expect, and anticipating some spectacular views. I'm really glad you're both here with me."

Later that day we drove to El Fuerte determined to take the only sensible way into the Canyon. We boarded *El Chepe*, the train that runs from coastal Los Mochis to Chihuahua City in the high desert. Two hours after leaving El Fuerte, the train crossed the longest bridge in Mexico, entered one of the valleys, and began to climb. As it gently ascended through the foothills, the glorious beauty of the Canyon soon began to reveal itself. For the next four hours my mouth was agape as we climbed through the narrow portal to our first stop. The engineering marvel of the track-bed hewn out of sheer granite never ceased to amaze us. The railway covers over 400 miles, climbs 8,000 feet into the Sierra Madres, and passes over 36 bridges and through 87 tunnels. Often we'd look straight down 1,000 feet to the bottom of the nearly dry river, and then look up thousands of feet to the top of the cliffs.

My son, an avid photographer, stood on the back of the train until the conductor told him he could not hang out over the end. None of his pleading persuaded them to let him keep his vantage point. Finally the machine gun-toting *policía*, hired to ensure safety of the travelers, convinced him that he would have to stick his head outside between cars. I would look back at Cal when the train doubled back and take pictures of him taking pictures of me taking pictures of him. It warmed me to be with him as a brother on a similar quest. It feels so good to see another at the point of their genius. He was in his element, eyes wide in wonder, drinking the scenery like a parched man who hadn't tasted water for eons.

Words can't describe the expansion in my heart when he and I gasped at yet another scenic collision of sky and cliff, or when tumbled boulders the size of small houses had dammed the river, creating large pools of water. In this dry season the green trees against the stark brown of the desert plant life stood out like searchlights. The rabid clicking of our shutters said it all. Later the three of us sat huddled over our cameras comparing what we'd captured.

Halfway to Creel, the train stops at Divisadero. This small settlement at the top of the ascent is the first opportunity the visitor has to be awed by the complete panorama of Copper Canyon. Food, tourist trinkets, and a few resorts offer the tourist a chance to get off the train and stand at the lip of a vista like nowhere else on earth. From here to the horizon all the traveler can see are the immense gashes in the earth as if some primordial six-toed beast had clawed its way through eons of time, creating a place for six rivers to join El Rio Fuerte (The Strong River).

I sat with my son and my wife on our balcony overlooking the stunning panorama. The spell of the sensuous swept over us. This is what had ignited me, grabbed my hand, whispered to some deep part, and called me out of the comfort of my home. This is what had goaded me through danger and physical pain to get as far as I did on my motorcycle trip. This breathtaking beauty was the same siren that had called my father out of the narrow canyon-like streets of Philadelphia to raise his family in the Madison Valley of Montana. This was the same siren that had called me forever to experience the most picturesque places in the world, that causes Gloria to stop in amazement before every giant tree she sees, that called my daughter to fall in love with Cape Town, South Africa, that called me to build our cabin on a serene lake in the Oregon coast range, and that pulls at my son to capture beauty through the lens of his camera. Holy places like this, seen or unseen, breathe life into the human soul.

While we sat with our complimentary margaritas, reminiscing about tongue-silencing vistas we'd visited in other parts of the world, a conversation I had with Calvin when he was in kindergarten came to mind. I'd just returned from my first men's conference, full of a new connection to the sacred masculine. By osmosis my burgeoning awareness of the deep current of masculine power deeply affected Calvin as well.

I looked up from that memory, "Cal, do you remember one day when you were a little kid you came into my shop while I was carving letter openers, sat on that wobbly stool and asked, 'Dad, when I am a father, will you give me some of these tools so I can give them to my son?'"

"Yeah, you've told me this story before."

"I don't know if I ever explained it all. I discovered something that day about what fathers are. Fathers are the portals through which the mysteries of life are passed on to the next generation. Now, here overlooking the Canyon, as I watch you frame this epiphany with delicate adjustments on your camera, capturing what words can never completely convey, I feel connected to the surging passion of three generations doing everything in our power to share the incomprehensible with the world. You never met my father, but the three of us are chiseled from the same piece of granite. Through your photography you're carrying on what my dad gave me when he taught me how to find agates in the mountains and rivers of Montana."

I remembered a poem I wrote for him shortly after that conversation and quoted it to him:

Calvin
Sometimes the shutters of your sleep
awaken the night's darkness
that hides the light you see in the day.
So you stumble up the stairs with
only your blanket to protect you
and whisper to me,
asking to be small in my embrace
so your courage can rest for awhile.
You speak a language that I know,
and my body graciously becomes a big ear
folding itself around you
and listens to what is passing
between us as we sleep.
I long for what I am giving
and say to you, my son,
my courage too
rests in something much greater.
What I give to you
is what I am given,
and when you ask
I discover what fathers are.

I don't think my father consciously infected me with beauty, but his adoration of nature awakened those feelings in me. I don't think I consciously set out to teach my children to adore it either, but Beauty herself pulled them to her through their longings to connect to something beyond them. Meister Eckhart said, "When the soul wishes to experience something, she throws an image out in front of her and then steps into her own image."

At dusk the three of us sat overlooking Copper Canyon with views that extended uninterrupted for more than 50 miles. Soaking in the life force of this geological marvel, I was at home. My eyes and my heart traced the ancient Tarahumara trails that snaked down the Canyon walls, descended from ledge to ledge, down vertigo-inducing cliffs all the way to the brown ribbon of the Urique River more than 6200 feet below, then zigzagged up the other side. Before me I faced the stark evidence of the river's erosive power that had sliced through multiple layers of solid granite, basalt, and mineral-rich stone, exposing 90 million years of geological history. I thought about human beings, and how, like the Canyon, their beauty is an amalgamation of what has been deposited and what has been shaped by watery power of the soul.

My arrival at this place was sweetened by my struggles to get here and the presence of Gloria and Cal who celebrated the same heart-opening moments with me. Both the human soul and the Canyon's heart are obscure treasures that aren't easy to find. The Siren of the Canyon had been singing to me for a long time. However, no one is ever simply given a proper map for the going in or the coming out. It must be earned. No one has traveled his or her individual path before, so the journey home becomes the map that must be lived in order to find the heart of the Canyon. When I finally arrived, She welcomed me as if I had come home again for the first time.

The edge of this map.

••